But thou, O Daniel, shut up the words, and seal the book, even to the time of the end

Daniel 12:4

When We Are

Revised Edition

A Logical Assessment of Bible Prophecy, the End Times, and the Second Coming of Christ

J C Farris

Contents

Preface to the Revised Edition

While most of this work has not changed, there were some places in which changes were needed. In order to be concise, I have taken out all of the text from the section on *The Seven Churches of Revelation* and replaced it with a comparative chronological table that highlights events in church history alongside the given order of the seven churches in that prophecy.

Also, within the two years since the first edition was published, I came upon some new revelation regarding the identity of the *restrainer* of 2nd Thessalonians 2, which I believe to be accurate. Rather than viewing it as some mysterious end-times prophecy as is taught in some theological circles, I have taken a more local and contextual approach. That entire section (*The Restrainer*) has been replaced with this new information (which is not really new, just rediscovered). This also led to some revision in the following section, *The Strong Delusion*.

Having reread the entire book several times, I made a few grammatical changes for easier reading. I have also added maps and some additional tables that were not included in the previous edition. It is my hope that this book, *When We Are,* serves to correct some serious errors of prophetic interpretation. It is also hoped to display the reality of God and His Word to a lost and dying world that desperately needs to turn to Him before it is too late.

Introduction

Our Place in Time

...for I am God, and there is none else; I am God, and there is none like me, declaring the end from the beginning, and from ancient times the things that are not yet done, saying, My counsel shall stand, and I will do all my pleasure - Isaiah 46:9-10

The story of this world has a definite beginning; and contrary to what seems to be popular opinion, it also has a predetermined ending. It is already written down in the Word of God; the Bible. And as certainly as its histories have been checked and verified, its fulfilled prophecies (now history) have been fulfilled to the letter.

These are not empty statements. The writings that make up the Bible have undergone more scrutiny than any other piece of literature ever written, by scholars great and small, both friendly and hostile. The countless studies, commentaries, scholarly works and new discoveries over the centuries have all contributed toward confirming the Bible as historically reliable and prophetically true.

But not all of the Bible's prophecies have been fulfilled. There is more to come. And as time presses forward, we are given to know that there are still things to look for along the way. We can look back to see where we've been, and we can also look forward to see what lies ahead. In this study, I am going to do my best, as precisely as possible, to mark our position on the timeline of God in relation to the coming of Christ; so that we can know *when we are*.

Not For Us to Know? Hindsight is 20/20!

Some believe that a study on the end times, or the second coming of Jesus Christ, is a waste of time. They normally tell us that it is not for us to know these things and that time would be better spent in other pursuits. However, Biblical scholars tell us that 25 to 30 percent of the Bible is eschatological (dealing with the time of the end).[i] But I believe this to be an understatement. On a quick search, I found over 30 eschatological references in the first ten chapters of the gospel of Matthew alone. So why would the Bible contain so much prophecy about the end times and the second coming of Jesus Christ if we are *not* to look into these things?

There are two quotes of Jesus that are normally used to make the point. So we'll have a look at those to see if they hold any validity. This first one from Matthew 24 follows a lengthy description by Jesus of events that will take place prior to His coming (see Matthew 24:5-31).

Matthew 24:36 But of that day and hour knoweth no man, no, not the angels of heaven, but my Father only.

A specific *day and hour* is not the same as all those events that Jesus had already mentioned that lead up to this verse; things that we *are* to look for, and things that He expected for us to *see*:

Matthew 24:33 So likewise ye, when ye shall see all these things, know that it is near, even at the doors.

We can know times and seasons without knowing the exact *day and hour*. So don't be discouraged.

The other verse is Acts 1:7, and is often misquoted to tell us that we cannot even know *the times or the seasons*. Let's look at that within its proper context, and see what it says.

Acts 1:6 When they therefore were come together, they asked of him, saying, Lord, wilt thou at this time restore again the kingdom to Israel?
1:7 And he said unto them, It is not for you to know the times or the seasons, which the Father hath put in his own power.
1:8 But ye shall receive power, after that the Holy Ghost is come upon you: and ye shall be witnesses unto me both in Jerusalem, and in all Judaea, and in Samaria, and unto the uttermost part of the earth.

Here we find Jesus answering a question His disciples had asked about restoring *the kingdom to Israel*. Apparently they had forgotten what He had said several times already. He said Jerusalem would be desolate (Matthew 23:37-38). He told them that not one stone would remain upon another that would not be thrown down (Matthew 24:2). You would think they would have gotten the message.

Rather than tell them the bad news all over again, Jesus merely said that it was not for them *to know the times or the seasons*. And it really wasn't for them to know; for they themselves became the dawn of *the times* and *seasons* that we look back on today. They would be the first of many who would tell the world what God had done through Jesus Christ on the cross. It took ages before the *times* and *seasons* could be recognizable. So it was not for them to know at that time. But after two thousand years, we have the hindsight, and it *is* for us to know.

Last Days Scoffers

2nd Peter 3:3 Knowing this first, that there shall come in the last days scoffers, walking after their own lusts,
3:4 And saying, Where is the promise of his coming? for since the fathers fell asleep, all things continue as they were from the beginning of the creation.

I have found that Bible prophecy, while informing us of things to come, doesn't normally tell us how or why these things will occur. We are merely told that they will happen. But we who are alive and experience them as they come upon us get to see how it all plays out during our lifetimes.

As we are moving closer in these latter days toward the very end, it is easy for us to look back and see why these *scoffers* would do what they do. And they make a good point. We need not go over every instance in history, but suffice it to say that there have been plenty of Christian leaders, as well as groups and cults of Christianity that have set dates for Christ's return, and all have failed. And so the *scoffers* come along, and scoff.

Note that these particular scoffers do not deny the Bible. They are not atheists. They confess *creation.* They mention the *fathers,* probably referring to people like Peter or John, or Paul, or what we might call the founding fathers of Christianity as we know it, having written the New Testament. And they have all fallen *asleep.* They all died a long time ago. And Jesus did not come.

The remarkable thing about Scripture is that through it, God has already dealt with people like these *scoffers.* He told us through Peter's words that they were coming before they ever arrived on the scene. And then Peter added this:

2nd Peter 3:8 But, beloved, be not ignorant of this one thing, that one day is with the Lord as a thousand years, and a thousand years as one day.
3:9 The Lord is not slack concerning his promise, as some men count slackness; but is longsuffering to us-ward, not willing that any should perish, but that all should come to repentance.

In other words, according to Peter, even though the LORD may come any day now, one day with Him may be a thousand years for us. And these *scoffers,* many of whom may be people we know personally, come to us in fulfillment of this prophecy. So rather than be drawn into joining them in their words, we should rejoice that God's Word has come to life in our presence, by *their* presence among us. For it is written that *there shall come in the last days, scoffers.* And here they are.

A Radical Departure

Although this book is a radical departure from some longstanding interpretations of Bible prophecy, the real *departures* (plural) actually took place long ago. And since they have never been recognized as the incorrect ideas that they are, they have grown over the centuries to become accepted standards among biblical scholars. So while this book may appear as if *it* is a departure, you will find it to be more in harmony with Scripture and that it better corresponds with history and reality as we know it.

Because so many books have been written (and continue to be written) that exploit Bible prophecy for profit, using current events to drive up hype for increased sales, my original intent was simply to provide a sober and rational study regarding where we are today on the prophetic timeline in relation to the return of Jesus Christ, without the hype and clutter. But in researching Daniel chapters 7 and 9, I inadvertently (perhaps providentially) stumbled upon some errors in Bible translation and prophetic interpretation that, because of their long and widespread acceptance, have actually hindered our understanding to more precisely grasp *when* we are, prophetically speaking. To further exacerbate the matter, we now have these long-established paradigms among biblical scholars, so that any other analysis will not easily be considered, regardless of its accuracy.

The problem of Daniel 7 is dealt with in Chapter 2 of this work. The difficulty in Daniel 9, however, is somewhat complex, and I want to tackle some of that now before we get into that section.

Misquoting Gabriel

When we read passages like those of Daniel 7 or Daniel 9, much of what we are reading are direct quotations of supernatural beings, or angels. Daniel 9:24-27 are the words of the angel Gabriel; and the early translators of the English Bible misquoted him.

The translators of the Geneva Bible of 1560, and subsequently those of the King James Bible of 1611, inserted an assumption into the text during the translation process. Scholarly insertions are not unusual. The *italicized* words in the King James Bible, for instance, are not found the original Greek or Hebrew texts, but were added to help us better understand the meaning of the original languages as expressed in English. In translating Daniel 9:25, however, the interpreters unintentionally misquoted Gabriel and set off a chain reaction of incorrect teaching that has wrongly directed our understanding of this prophecy. Note that Gabriel specifically mentioned two timelines; two sets of *weeks:*

Daniel 9:25 Know therefore and understand, that from the going forth of the commandment to restore and to build Jerusalem unto the Messiah the Prince shall be seven weeks, and threescore and two weeks: … 9:26 And after threescore and two weeks shall Messiah be cut off, but not for himself: and the people of the prince that shall come shall destroy the city and the sanctuary...

The text here is from the King James Version of 1611. Note the two sets of weeks: *seven weeks, and threescore and two weeks.* There can be no mistaking the division between the two: seven weeks, and sixty-two weeks. That's the way the Hebrew has it as well. There is no misquote here.

Now note the capital letters in verse 25, *Messiah the Prince.* This is the misquote. The Hebrew text is not so specific as the King James has it here. It merely reads, *an anointed one, a leader.*[ii] Likewise, the Hebrew of verse 26 reads *an anointed one* and does not specify who this *anointed one* is. Had the early English translators merely left the words as they are, we might have understood the possibility of *two* anointed ones, or an anointed one and a *coming leader*: one arriving at the end of the seven weeks, and the other fulfilled at the end of the sixty-two weeks.

But because these English translators of 1560 and 1611 knew that Jesus was the *anointed one* who would be *cut off* (or killed) in verse 26, they assumed that both verses (25 and 26) referred to Jesus and inserted the capital letters into both, thus changing what Gabriel actually said. Also, the people of those days only knew of one time in history in which the Jews had returned to Jerusalem after being exiled, with only one *commandment to restore and to build* their city. Working with partial knowledge, the people of that era had no idea that in about 400 years, Jerusalem would once again be restored to the Jews.

The second appearance of Israel and Jerusalem together again allows for the two timelines that Gabriel specified, with two different fulfillments by two different people. But the translators of those days would not have understood this. Neither did they understand that they themselves were living during an age of unfolding biblical prophecy. They were living in the dawn of the fourth beast of Daniel 7 (see Chapter 2 of this book).

Their intentions were good, but the insertions misguided. Much like the rudder of a boat, even slightly tweaked, will guide it to a wrong destination, our *ship* of prophetic understanding was sent off course. To make matters worse, even the more recent translations such as the *New American Standard Bible*, the *New International Version*, the *Christian Standard Bible* and others, also followed suit with the capital letters (I found this also in some of the Spanish translations).

And herein we find our problem. By assuming Jesus as the fulfillment of the entire prophecy in Daniel 9:25-26, and inserting that assumption into verse 25 with the capital letters (*Messiah the Prince*), it forced scholars to bring together into one, the two separate timelines (the *seven weeks* and the *threescore and two weeks* of Dan. 9:25), which Gabriel did not do, thereby departing from accurately interpreting the text.

This led researchers to try and explain how the first advent of Jesus fulfilled the two different time spans which have been combined into one; because it simply doesn't fit. That amount of years takes us past His birth, and well into or beyond His earthly ministry (depending on how the years are calculated).

And so we have differences of opinions and various calculations, each with an explanation as to how this or that hypothesis is worthy of our consideration.[iii] And none of this may ever have been an issue had the early English translators simply allowed Gabriel to say what he said: *an anointed one, a leader*.

Although some of the more recent translations have corrected this error,[iv] a process had already begun and developed into centuries of scholarly work, teaching aids, and commentaries that assume the first advent of Jesus Christ as the fulfillment of two separate timelines which have been combined into one. And it continues to this day.

So keep these things in mind when reading this book. You are not going to find the traditional, centuries-old explanations of some major prophecies here. This is a radical departure from the accepted norm of "the way we've always interpreted it" (while ignoring the problems created thereby).

This work is the result of seriously looking into the problems, asking the questions to understand how those problems came about, and finding answers to better understand the message of Scripture as it relates to the world in which we are familiar. Consequently, you will likely learn how real God is as you see Bible prophecy unfold over time to match our own history books, as recent as the twenty-first century, with more yet to come. Like truth, it will resonate with reality; and you will learn *when we are*.

Final Introductory Notes

On Multiple Bible Translations

While the King James text is used throughout this work, there are some passages in which other English translations are necessary, for two reasons. One reason is simply for clarity in understanding. The King James Bible is archaic, and some of its words and phrases are outmoded. They are no longer used, and therefore not easily understood. In those cases I have chosen English translations that more clearly express the point of the passage quoted, in order to maintain a measure of simplicity for the reader.

The other reason is for those passages that demand greater accuracy to the original language than the King James translation provides, as pointed out in the previous section. Those instances are explained wherever this becomes an issue.

Be Aware

This is a Christian work. This is a biblical work. It assumes a true Bible and holds to a biblical Christian belief system. As such, it will be in agreement with all biblical definitions of sin. Some may find this unpleasant, but as stated, this is a biblically based book, and attempts to agree with the Bible on every point.

Chapter 1

Daniel 2: A Chronology of Kingdoms

Introduction

Daniel 2 is one of the greatest examples of prophecy in God's Word. It tells of four empires that were coming. Most of it is history for us today. But in 600 BC, when Daniel wrote it all down, it was prophetic. Of the four empires mentioned, one was already dominant: Babylon. The others had not yet risen to prominence at the time that this prophecy was written.

These empires would span the ages from the days of Babylon (Daniel's time) all the way to the end, when God's kingdom comes. I said that it was *mostly* history for us today, because there is more to come; and we were told about it long ago, here in Daniel 2. In other words, we are living in a story that was already written.

This particular prophecy was packaged inside a dream; a king's dream. In his dream, King Nebuchadnezzar of Babylon saw a great image in human form. It had a head of gold, chest and arms of silver, belly and thighs of brass (or bronze, depending on the English translation you are using), legs of iron, with its feet and toes a mix of iron and clay (2:31-33).

The king knew that he had seen something profound, and he wanted to know what it meant. God revealed both the dream and the meaning of it to Daniel and his companions. Daniel told the king; and this has been preserved in writing through the ages so that we may know Him who reveals the end from the beginning.

The Prophecy

The King's Dream

Daniel 2:31 Thou, O king, sawest, and behold a great image. This great image, whose brightness was excellent, stood before thee; and the form thereof was terrible.
2:32 This image's head was of fine gold, his breast and his arms of silver, his belly and his thighs of brass,
2:33 His legs of iron, his feet part of iron and part of clay.

Daniel's Interpretation

Daniel 2:36 This is the dream; and we will tell the interpretation thereof before the king.
2:37 Thou, O king, art a king of kings: for the God of heaven hath given thee a kingdom, power, and strength, and glory.
2:38 And wheresoever the children of men dwell, the beasts of the field and the fowls of the heaven hath he given into thine hand, and hath made thee ruler over them all. Thou art this head of gold.
2:39 And after thee shall arise another kingdom inferior to thee, and another third kingdom of brass [or bronze], which shall bear rule over all the earth.
2:40 And the fourth kingdom shall be strong as iron: forasmuch as iron breaketh in pieces and subdueth all things: and as iron that breaketh all these, shall it break in pieces and bruise.

*2:41 And whereas thou sawest the feet and toes, part of potters'
clay, and part of iron, the kingdom shall be divided; but there shall
be in it of the strength of the iron, forasmuch as thou sawest the
iron mixed with miry clay.
2:42 And as the toes of the feet were part of iron, and part of
clay, so the kingdom shall be partly strong, and partly broken.*

In this prophecy, we are given to know that the *head of gold*
represents Babylon (2:38). While the others are not made known
here in this chapter, we have the order in which they would rise
to prominence. And so we learn from Daniel chapter 5, and from
history, that the Medes and Persians would overthrow Babylon
(5:28), making the Medio-Persian Empire the fulfillment of the
breast and arms of *silver*.

And then, in Daniel 8, in the vision of the ram and the male goat
(8:20-21), we find that Greece is the third kingdom (the *brass*
portion of the image). This is also history. Three of the four
kingdoms in Nebuchadnezzar's image are revealed by name in the
book of Daniel. Although the fourth kingdom is not identified,
history tells us that it is the Roman Empire.

Historically, we understand these empires to be Babylon (*gold*),
Medio-Persia (*silver*), Greece (*brass* or *bronze*, translations vary),
Rome (*iron*), and Rome divided (*iron and clay*). As Daniel
described, each was succeeded by the following empire: Babylon
fell to Medio-Persia, which fell to the Greek empire under
Alexander. The four-fold division of the Greek empire after
Alexander's death is prophetically described in Daniel 8 through
the imagery of the horns on the male goat. But those kingdoms all
fell to the Romans.

Rome (*iron* - 2:40) was not conquered by another nation, but became divided and fell apart (*part of iron and part of clay* - 2:41). There is a reason for selecting these kingdoms out of all the kingdoms of the earth. They each directly affected God's chosen people – the Jews.

Keep in mind that this prophecy was written about 70 years before the Medes and Persians conquered Babylon, about 300 years before Persia would fall to the Greeks, about 500 years before the Romans took over, and roughly a thousand years before the Roman Empire divided and fell apart. And Daniel credits God for providing this foreknowledge (Daniel 2:28, 45).

Nebuchadnezzar's Image:
A Chronology of Kingdoms[1]

Head of Gold:
Babylon
605-539 BC

Chest and Arms of Silver
Medio-Persia
550-330 BC

Belly and thighs of Bronze
Greece
330-146 BC

Legs of Iron
Rome
150 BC-AD 476

Feet and Toes of
Iron and Clay:
The Divided Roman Empire
AD 476 - Present

---

[1] Dates are approximate.

The Stumbling Stone

There is another piece of that dream I did not mention. It's not part of that various-metaled statue, but it is part of Nebuchadnezzar's dream. It is a *stone*; a stone cut from a mountain, *cut out without hands* (or without human means). The stone destroys the image.

Daniel 2:34 Thou sawest till that a stone was cut out without hands, which smote the image upon his feet that were of iron and clay, and brake them to pieces.
2:35 Then was the iron, the clay, the brass, the silver, and the gold, broken to pieces together, and became like the chaff of the summer threshingfloors; and the wind carried them away, that no place was found for them: and the stone that smote the image became a great mountain, and filled the whole earth.

Daniel revealed the meaning of the stone.

Daniel 2:43 And whereas thou sawest iron mixed with miry clay, they shall mingle themselves with the seed of men: but they shall not cleave one to another, even as iron is not mixed with clay.
2:44 And in the days of these kings shall the God of heaven set up a kingdom, which shall never be destroyed: and the kingdom shall not be left to other people, but it shall break in pieces and consume all these kingdoms, and it shall stand for ever.
2:45 Forasmuch as thou sawest that the stone was cut out of the mountain without hands, and that it brake in pieces the iron, the brass, the clay, the silver, and the gold; ...

From the time that the Roman Empire divided and fell apart until now, we have been in the days of the *iron and clay*. The time of the *stone* is coming. It is next. The *stone* is something other than and outside of Nebuchadnezzar's image. It is separate from the nations of this world. It strikes the image at the feet and toes: our part on the timeline. It destroys the image completely and grows to fill *the whole earth*. This portion of the prophecy has not yet happened. But we know as a fact of Scripture that Jesus Christ is coming to judge the world and establish God's kingdom. When He arrives, the kingdoms of this world will fall.

Revelation 11:15 And the seventh angel sounded; and there were great voices in heaven, saying, "The kingdoms of this world are become the kingdoms of our Lord, and of his Christ; and he shall reign for ever and ever."

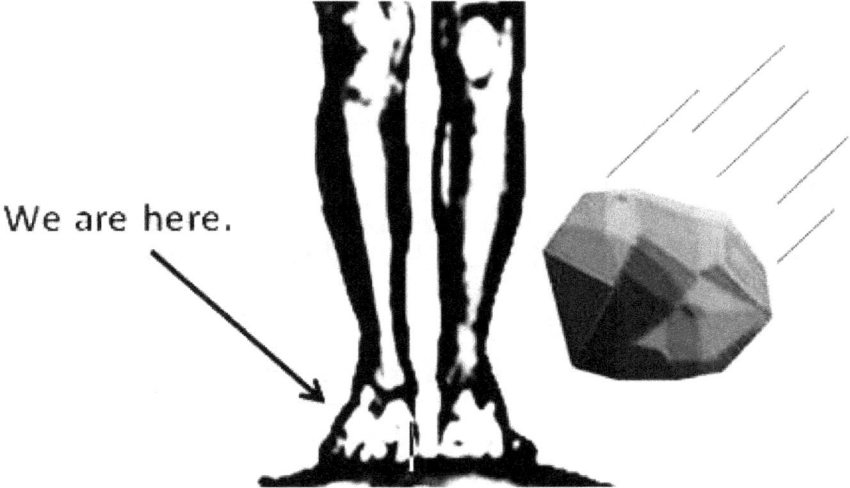

We are here.

23

Chapter 2

Daniel 7: The Four Beasts

The Traditional Interpretation with its Problems

The Texts

Daniel 7:3 And four great beasts came up from the sea, diverse one from another.

7:4 The first was like a lion, and had eagle's wings: I beheld till the wings thereof were plucked, and it was lifted up from the earth, and made stand upon the feet as a man, and a man's heart was given to it.

7:5 And behold another beast, a second, like to a bear, and it raised up itself on one side, and it had three ribs in the mouth of it between the teeth of it: and they said thus unto it, Arise, devour much flesh.

7:6 After this I beheld, and lo another, like a leopard, which had upon the back of it four wings of a fowl; the beast had also four heads; and dominion was given to it.

7:7 After this I saw in the night visions, and behold a fourth beast, dreadful and terrible, and strong exceedingly; and it had great iron teeth: it devoured and brake in pieces, and stamped the residue with the feet of it: and it was diverse from all the beasts that were before it; and it had ten horns.

Daniel 7:17 These great beasts, which are four, are four kings, which shall arise out of the earth.

Shattering My Paradigm

By 2011, I had studied the Bible and Bible prophecy for about thirty years, and was comfortable with the established consensus on the identities of these four beasts as handed down by the scholars; that they represented the same kingdoms of Daniel 2: Babylon, Medio-Persia, Greece, and Rome. Open up any reputable, conservative Bible commentary and that's what you're likely to find. And while other ideas have been suggested,[v] this model made the most sense, in that it best reflected what we know from history.

This explanation dates back to and likely originated with an early church father named Hippolytus.[vi] He lived around the years 170-236, and it seems that his analysis became the standard throughout history to this day. Working from his standpoint in history, it was a very convincing conclusion.

But Hippolytus lived at a time during which prophecy was still unfolding. Rome was not yet divided in his day (as foretold in Daniel 2). Nearly two thousand years has passed since the days of Hippolytus. Other empires have come and gone from his time to our time, and it appears that Daniel's prophecy looked further ahead than Hippolytus (and many others) realized.

This may be a good place to point out two notable problems with this traditional view of the four beasts. First and foremost is the phrase in verse 17, *shall arise*[vii]:

Daniel 7:17 These great beasts, which are four, are four kings, which shall arise out of the earth.

Though I had read it time and again, as scholars and biblical expositors have for centuries, I completely missed it, as some of them likely did. It took someone else to point it out to me; an elderly Pentecostal woman named *Renee* (her user name on an internet Christian discussion forum). Renee's interpretation of the passage was more contemporary, making England out to be the lion, with modern nations like Russia and the United States to fill in for the other beasts. As I don't advocate for "making prophecy fit" into our times, I "corrected" her with the standard explanation: Babylon, Medio-Persia, Greece, and Rome. But then Renee pointed out those two small but powerful words from verse 17: *shall arise*.

Daniel was in Babylon when he had the vision. Babylon had already risen. It was not a kingdom yet to come, as the beasts of the vision, which *shall arise*. Therefore, Babylon could not be the lion.

Another problem is found in verses 11-12, where we are told what happens to the fourth beast:

I beheld even till the beast was slain, and his body destroyed, and given to the burning flame. As concerning the rest of the beasts, they had their dominion taken away: yet their lives were prolonged for a season and time. Daniel 7:11-12

The passage says that the *fourth beast* will be destroyed, while the first three *beasts* would continue to exist *for a season and time*. Those first three beasts include the lion. Since we know from Scripture that Babylon will be destroyed at the return of Christ, the lion cannot be representative of Babylon.

Revelation 18:21 And a mighty angel took up a stone like a great millstone, and cast it into the sea, saying, Thus with violence shall that great city Babylon be thrown down, and shall be found no more at all.

Upon realizing that our "standard" explanation was very likely in error, I began to search the great empires of world history for other possible candidates. This took time. Nothing seemed to fit. So I changed my focus and began to concentrate on the imagery of those four beasts, down the fine details of each one.

In my mind's eye I saw the *wings plucked* from the *lion*. It stood up to become a man. And something I had learned from history occurred to me, which made sense. I checked the next empire, the *bear* with *one side raised up*. It matched. Each beast, down to the fine details, perfectly reflected the progression from one empire to the next. It all fell into place, and thanks to the internet and the use of search engines, it took less than an hour.

Daniel 7 Interpretation: Proposed Revision

Tradition can often be like a door that is shut; covering a portal of unfathomable truth. Do you want Scripture to come alive? Open the door. Move the tradition aside, and you just might see what you have been missing. What you are about to read will give you a completely different, yet accurate perspective on the book of Daniel.

Recall that Daniel chapter 2 provides a prophetic overview of four kingdoms through the imagery of Nebuchadnezzar's dream. We saw that Daniel identified the first kingdom, revealing Babylon as the head of gold (2:37-38).

In Daniel chapter 5, we learned the identity of the second kingdom when Babylon was conquered by the Medio-Persian alliance (the silver of Daniel 2). And in chapter 8, through Daniel's vision of the Ram and the He-Goat, the third kingdom of brass is revealed to be Greece (8:21).

The fourth kingdom of iron (that becomes divided into iron and clay) is never identified; nor do we learn anything else about it in the book of Daniel. Or did we miss something?

Hippolytus and others throughout history didn't see it, because they *couldn't* see it. They were living in it as it was occurring. And it took about 2,000 years to unfold. Modern Bible scholars haven't seen it either, because they never looked for it. They were already told that the four beasts represented Babylon, Medio-Persia, Greece and Rome. So they merely accepted that information and passed it on to the rest of us without looking any further. And maybe it was meant to be that way.

Daniel 12:4 But thou, O Daniel, shut up the words, and seal the book, even to the time of the end.

What I am proposing is that Daniel, in chapter 7, rather than restating Daniel 2 all over again but in a different way, zooms in on that fourth kingdom of iron, and iron mixed with clay (as chapter 8 does for the second and third kingdoms of Nebuchadnezzar's image). With hindsight as our guide, the beasts of Daniel 7 will come to life. Prophecy will rise from the pages of Scripture to transport us through a known and real history without obscurity; from the Roman Republic to European global colonization, and everything in between.

The First Three Beasts: Revised Interpretation

The First Beast: Rome

Daniel 7:4 The first was like a lion, and had eagle's wings: I beheld till the wings thereof were plucked, and it was lifted up from the earth, and made stand upon the feet as a man, and a man's heart was given to it.

As a city, Rome began as a monarchy with a king, as cities did in ancient times. It became a republic not long after Daniel's time, with its government run by a senate. This begins the period of the legs of iron in Daniel 2. It is noteworthy to add that Rome was not much different from other successful empires of those times. This is important, because the *fourth beast* will be very different from the others (Dan. 7:7, 19. Verse 23 is even more emphatic: it will be different from *all kingdoms*). All of the ancient empires used swords, spears, catapults, bows and arrows. They all used horses and chariots. Rome was no exception. Rome struggled for dominance, and once obtained, Rome struggled to keep it. *Different* is not the defining characteristic of the Roman Empire. But something very different would certainly happen here.

By about 50 BC, Rome's dominion spread over Europe as far west as Spain, included much of North Africa, and stretched into Asia Minor. If the *eagle's wings* (a driving force) were represented by the Roman Senate, they were *plucked,* when in 44 BC, Julius Caesar declared himself *dictator perpetuo* (dictator for life). From that time forward Rome was ruled by one *man*: Caesar.

But there is another way to apply the imagery, which is also the different thing that happened in the Roman Empire that never happened before or since anywhere else. For if the strength of a nation is found in the common religion (belief system) of its people, the Romans worshiped many gods. It was to this world within the Roman Empire that God entered: in the Person of Jesus Christ. With the advent of Christianity, the idols and gods that Rome acknowledged were *plucked* up.

Note that the lion is the only one of the four beasts that is physically changed by something outside of itself. *It was lifted up from the earth, and made stand upon the feet as a man, and a man's heart was given to it*. A new age had begun. A new and different Spirit had entered into the world; and with that Spirit, the new man.

The Roman Empire encompassed the land mass surrounding the Mediterranean: Europe, North Africa, and eastward into the Middle East and Asia Minor. What happens next is the breaking up of that region into other kingdoms (see Daniel 2:41-43). This division will move in a clockwise direction: east, then south and west, and then back to the north with Rome once again playing a dominant role.

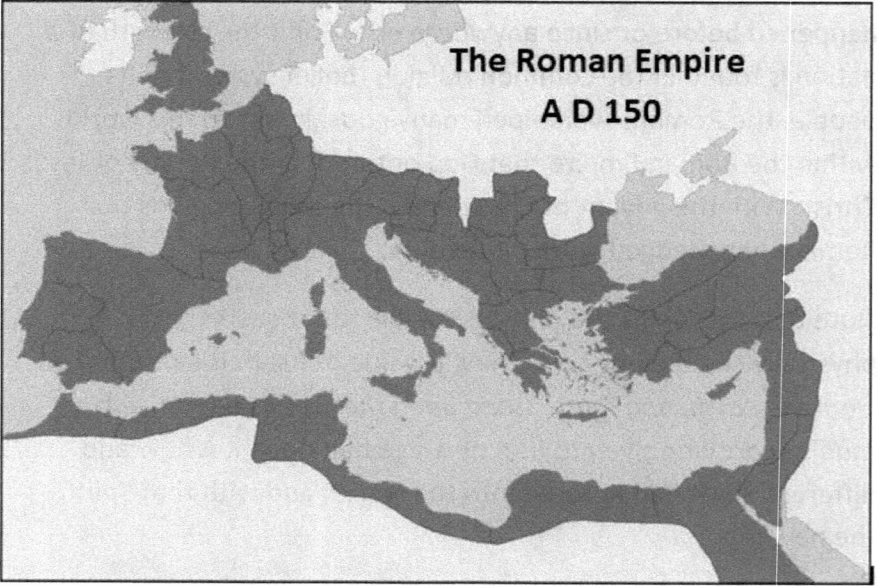

The First Beast of Daniel 7 – The Roman Empire

The Second Beast: The Byzantine Empire

Daniel 7:5 And behold another beast, a second, like to a bear, and it raised up itself on one side, and it had three ribs in the mouth of it between the teeth of it: and they said thus unto it, Arise, devour much flesh.

In AD 330, Roman Emperor Constantine moved the capital from Rome eastward to Byzantium, and changed the name of that city to Constantinople, in what is now Turkey. While the western part of the empire began to wane and fall apart, Constantinople and the eastern empire would continue on into the next millennium, and was later known as the Byzantine Empire. This would correspond to the raised side of the *bear* (as the western empire corresponds to the side not risen or maybe unable to rise).

The *three ribs* between its teeth might represent Anatolia (Turkey), Greece and Italy, over which the Byzantine Empire originally stretched. Or they might represent, over the longer term, Turkey, Greece and Russia. Russia was heavily influenced by Byzantium, and still is to this day.

But it is more likely that the ribs represent cities. Biblically, cities are referred to in the feminine, making the ribs (Eve was created from Adam's rib) an appropriate reference to cities. This *bear*, which rose up out of *Rome*, reigned for a thousand years from *Constantinople* (its risen side), and continued on after the fall of Constantinople through Byzantine influence over Russia, from *Moscow*. Moscow was referred to as the "third Rome" after the fall of Constantinople.

The command to *arise and devour much flesh* may be indicative of a sickly condition, as one might be told to get up and eat in order to regain health and strength after an illness. Half of the empire was falling apart, and this second beast marks the beginning of the divided kingdom of Daniel 2:41.

The Second Beast: The first division of the Roman Empire. By this point in history, Rome (to the west) is in decline, while Byzantium, (renamed Constantinople) will remain for about a thousand years.

(Map from Wikimedia Commons. Licensed under the Creative Commons Attribution-Share Alike 3.0 Unpurported license.
https://commons.wikimedia.org/wiki/File:Map_of_the_Byzantine_Empire,_10
25_AD.svg)

The Third Beast: The Islamic Empire

Daniel 7:6 After this I beheld, and lo another, like a leopard, which had upon the back of it four wings of a fowl; the beast had also four heads; and dominion was given to it.

Swiftness and unpredictability is descriptive of the leopard, and also of the rise of Islam. The quick, multidirectional conquests for which early Islam is famous compares well to the leopard with four wings. Under the Rashidun,[viii] the first *four* caliphs of Islam (the four wings?), Muslims gained control of Egypt to the west, invaded eastward to conquer all of Persia, and northward as far as the Black Sea, all within forty years.

But the Rashidun was only the first of *four* lines, or kingdoms, of Islam (the four heads of the leopard). The Umayyad Dynasty[ix] would replace the Rashidun, and gain the entirety of North Africa, cross over into Spain, to be finally stopped in 732 by Charles Martel of the Franks (grandfather to Charlemagne – first emperor of the Holy Roman Empire).

The Abbasid Dynasty[x] was next. Known as the "Golden Age of Islam," it lasted five hundred years; until 1258, when it was overtaken by Islamic kingdom number four: the Ottoman Empire. This fourth and final *head* of the *leopard* stood for nearly 700 years, taking us into the twentieth century, and finally ending with the close of World War I.

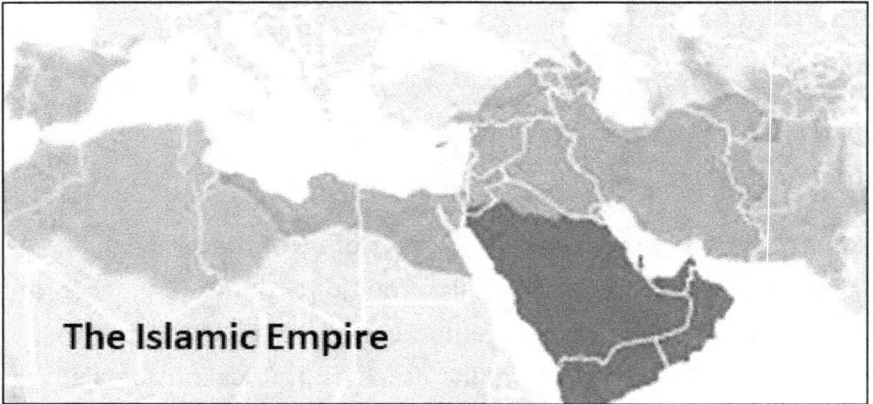

The Islamic Empire

The Third Beast: Further division of the Roman Empire. This map shows the division of Islam through its first three caliphates. The fourth caliphate will be the Ottoman Empire, which will overthrow Byzantium, and change the name of Constantinople to Istanbul.

The Fourth Beast: Globalism - European Colonialism and the "New World" Order

The Texts

Daniel 7:7 After this I saw in the night visions, and behold a fourth beast, dreadful and terrible, and strong exceedingly; and it had great iron teeth: it devoured and brake in pieces, and stamped the residue with the feet of it: and it was diverse from all the beasts that were before it; and it had ten horns.
7:8 I considered the horns, and, behold, there came up among them another little horn, before whom there were three of the first horns plucked up by the roots: and, behold, in this horn were eyes like the eyes of man, and a mouth speaking great things.

7:23 Thus he said, The fourth beast shall be the fourth kingdom upon earth, which shall be diverse from all kingdoms, and shall devour the whole earth, and shall tread it down, and break it in pieces.
7:24 And the ten horns out of this kingdom are ten kings that shall arise: and another shall rise after them; and he shall be diverse from the first, and he shall subdue three kings.

The Fourth Beast: Different from all Kingdoms

Different is a one-word description of this *fourth beast*; it *shall be diverse from all kingdoms*. Unlike the other three beasts, Daniel could not compare this one to any known creature on earth.

And so we begin this *fourth kingdom* in Europe, about the time of Charlemagne. Charlemagne was crowned by the pope in AD 800 as emperor of the Holy Roman Empire. The west had gained new life, but the joining together of its nation-states proved difficult, if not impossible. Throughout their turbulent history, these so-called "Christian" nations of Europe, though connected by one religion, were continually warring with each other. Internally, they terrorized their own citizens under the banner of the cross, as Christians were persecuted by what was called, "the Church."

It was this disjointed body of warring factions that, beginning in 1492, would set out to *devour the whole earth*. As with the other beasts, this beast will also span the centuries, and we are still in it today. From the beginning of its conquests, technology provided the *iron* which enabled these disorganized European states (as *iron and clay*, not adhering to each other – Dan. 2:43) to *devour the whole earth, tread it down, and break it in pieces*. Spears, bows and catapults were no match against the iron: guns and canons. The power of the printing press (Germany, ca 1450) should not be underestimated, as it facilitated a more rapid pace in mass communication, education and propaganda.

With this *fourth beast* also came the machines: steam powered trains and steamships, wire communication and electricity, radio, cars, aircraft, aircraft carriers, photography and motion pictures, television, nuclear weapons and missile technology, nuclear powered submarines, lasers, drones, satellites and space probes, the Internet, cell phones, etc. – making this *fourth beast* and our times completely and absolutely *different from all kingdoms*; different from anything this world has ever seen.

Daniel 7:24 - The Horns of the Beast: Conquering Kingdoms

Daniel 7:24 And the ten horns out of this kingdom are ten kings that shall arise: and another shall rise after them; and he shall be diverse from the first, and he shall subdue three kings.

The horns are revealed to be kings, but we are not told anything else about them. Many conservative scholars link these ten kings of Daniel to the ten kings of Revelation 17:12 (also represented by 10 horns), but there are noteworthy differences. The beast of Revelation has seven heads. This one does not. The ten kings of Revelation do not have another king rising up after them to subdue three kings, as we have here in Daniel. Revelation's kings will reign together at the very end and will make war with the Lamb, only to meet their demise (Revelation 17:12-14). But Daniel's fourth beast, in its devouring, treading down, and dividing the whole earth presents a history that is mostly behind us (though prophetic at the time of writing). This is a different beast, and its horns are a part of its message; possibly indicating how and by whom the world would *be devoured, trodden down, and broken in pieces.*

Looking back into the days of European colonization, we find that there were indeed ten kingdoms that took part in devouring the whole earth: Portugal, Spain, the Netherlands (Dutch), France, England, Denmark/ Norway[xi], Sweden, Belgium, Germany and Italy[xii]. That makes ten nations out of the fourth beast that colonized the world. They literally divided it up.

When We Are

This global colonizing is very likely a partial fulfillment of Daniel 7:24; but there is this other king that *shall arise after them*. We are not told how long *after them* he *shall arise;* and while it does not appear that he has arrived yet, he is coming. His reservation is in order, and the world is currently in preparation for his arrival.

Up to this point, we have seen Daniel's vision of the four beasts come to life through the kingdoms that rose from the same geographical region that was once the Roman Empire. Prophetic at the time of writing, it is now history. If hindsight is 20/20, we can truly say that prophecy has been fulfilled before our eyes.

Most recent are the ten European nations that colonized, or *devoured the whole earth*, corresponding to the *ten horns* of this fourth and final beast. Those years of global colonization are behind us now. In 1999, Portugal relinquished its sovereignty over Macau, the last of the European colonies. This is where we are today, or *when* we are. We are still in the same beast, but at a point after those ten horns, and before that *little horn* to come, placing us near the edge of the end of this world as we know it.

The Fourth Beast and Its Horns, or Europe and Its Colonizing Kingdoms

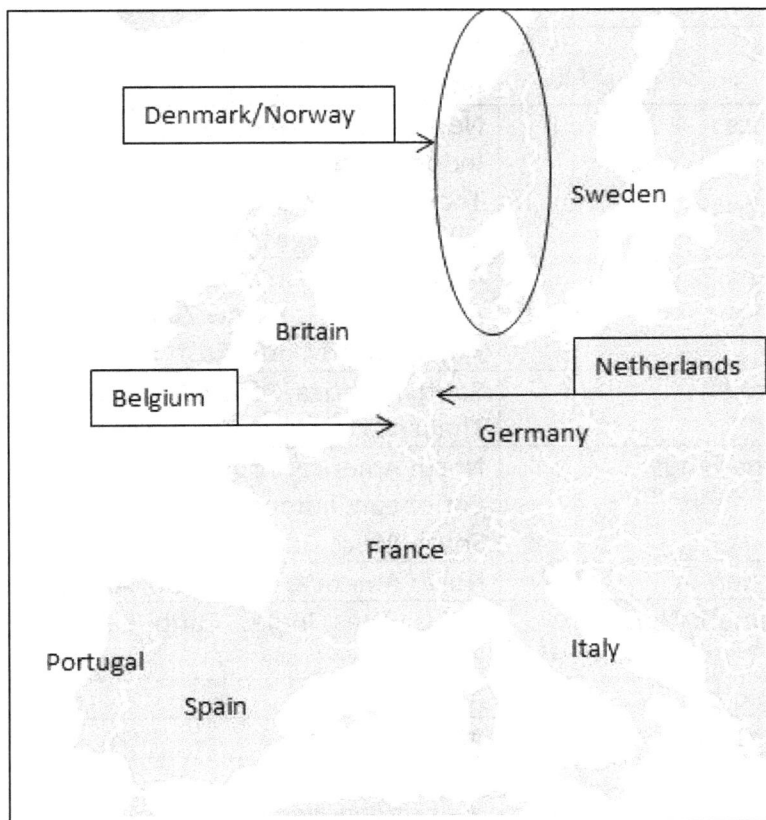

The Fourth Beast Devours the whole World

Horns of the Beast	Whole World Devoured and Broken in Pieces
Spain	North, Central and South America, Philippines, Spanish East Indies
France	North and South America, Africa, French Indochina (Cambodia, Laos, Myanmar, Thailand, Vietnam, Malaysia), Caribbean Islands, Madagascar
Britain	North, Central and South America, Australia, Africa, New Zealand, India, Hong Kong, Middle East
Portugal	South America, Africa, China, India, Thailand
Netherlands	North America, South America, Caribbean, Indonesia, India, Taiwan, South Africa, Japan*
Sweden	North America, Caribbean, Africa, India
Denmark/Norway	Danish West Indies (Caribbean), Africa, India
Belgium	Africa
Germany	Africa
Italy	Africa

*Although Japan was not colonized, the Dutch maintained a trading post at Nagasaki. Japan would later succumb to the Fourth Beast by the end of World War II.

The process has been ongoing. France and Britain, in aiding the Turks, defeated Russia in the Crimean War of the 19th century. These same two "horns" also gained territory in the Middle East once held by the Ottoman Empire at the close of World War I. United Nations forces fought against Communist armies in Korea in the 20th century, and in our own century, the British and U.S. waged war and defeated Iraq and Afghanistan. This Fourth Beast has truly devoured the whole earth, has tread it down (under the feet of its troops), and has broken it in pieces, (Daniel 7:23-24).

The Little Horn

The Texts

Daniel 7:8 I considered the horns, and, behold, there came up among them another little horn, before whom there were three of the first horns plucked up by the roots: and, behold, in this horn were eyes like the eyes of man, and a mouth speaking great things.

Daniel 7:21 I beheld, and the same horn made war with the saints, and prevailed against them;
7:22 Until the Ancient of days came, and judgment was given to the saints of the most High; and the time came that the saints possessed the kingdom.

Daniel 7:24 And the ten horns out of this kingdom are ten kings that shall arise: and another shall rise after them; and he shall be diverse from the first, and he shall subdue three kings.
7:25 And he shall speak great words against the most High, and shall wear out the saints of the most High, and think to change times and laws: and they shall be given into his hand until a time and times and the dividing of time.
7:26 But the judgment shall sit, and they shall take away his dominion, to consume and to destroy it unto the end.
7:27 And the kingdom and dominion, and the greatness of the kingdom under the whole heaven, shall be given to the people of the saints of the most High, whose kingdom is an everlasting kingdom, and all dominions shall serve and obey him.

These verses provide a lot of information about this *little horn.*
Verse 24 tells us that it will rise up *after* the first *ten horns* (or
kings), but we are not told how long after these kings he would
arrive. And as the *fourth beast* was different from the other
beasts, it says that this king will also be different from the other
kings; he will be *diverse from the first.*

We are told that he will have a *mouth speaking great things* (7:8).
He will speak *great words against the most High* and that he will
wear out the saints of the most High (v. 25). He will also seek *to
change times and laws* (v. 25). He will make *war with the saints*
(the people of God), and will defeat them. But in verse 22 it says,
until. His victory will not be a lasting one.

*Daniel 7:21 I beheld, and the same horn made war with the
saints, and prevailed against them;
7:22 Until the Ancient of days came...*

In other words, this *little horn* will be the final king according to
Bible prophecy. His reign will end at the arrival of God's kingdom.

At the time of this writing, this *little horn* king has either not yet
arrived, or if he has, he has not yet been made known. There is no
nation or world leader known for openly speaking *great words*
against God as this *little horn* king will do. But it seems things are
headed in that direction; and we have also sailed into uncharted
waters (unfulfilled prophecy).

Conclusion

While we are given some things to look for as we move forward into the unknown, we are not given specifics as to how these things will play out. Nobody recognized the four beasts as they rose during the times that they were rising. And none of the biblical scholars understood, as the European nations colonized the world, that they were living under the fulfillment of the horns of the fourth beast. For us today, all of this is hindsight, or *charted* territory (see the table at the end of this chapter). This portion of the prophecy ended in the twentieth century when European colonization ceased. We mark its official ending in 1999 when Portugal transferred sovereignty of the last European colony, Macau, to China.

But this *fourth beast* hasn't gone anywhere, and we are still living in it today. It's *when we are*. Our place now is after those years of global conquest, and before or at the time that this other *little horn* begins his reign. God's Word has not left us in the dark, and Daniel's vision provides some identifiers to look for so that we can recognize him when he gets here.

It says that he shall *think to change times and laws: and they shall be given into his hand*. The last century has seen something like this, as special *times* like Christmas and Easter have been transformed to become the Holiday Season and Spring Break. And our standard for numbering the years is being revised. The old BC (Before Christ) and AD (*Anno Domini,* Latin for "In the Year of Our Lord") is being changed to BCE (Before the Common Era) and ACE (After the Common Era). The prince of this world obviously has a problem with Jesus and seeks to erase His Name.

Laws are also undergoing change. Preferential treatment favoring race and sexual license over real issues of right and wrong, under the pretense of inequality and "social justice," is becoming a rule of law in our time. Sin is openly practiced, celebrated, and legally protected. And the world, still following the lead of Western powers (the fourth beast), is moving toward its goal to become one global community, creating new laws that the whole world is expected to follow. According to biblical standards, it appears that Satan himself is preparing this world for the arrival of his coming leader. The little horn is next, and after that the end will come.

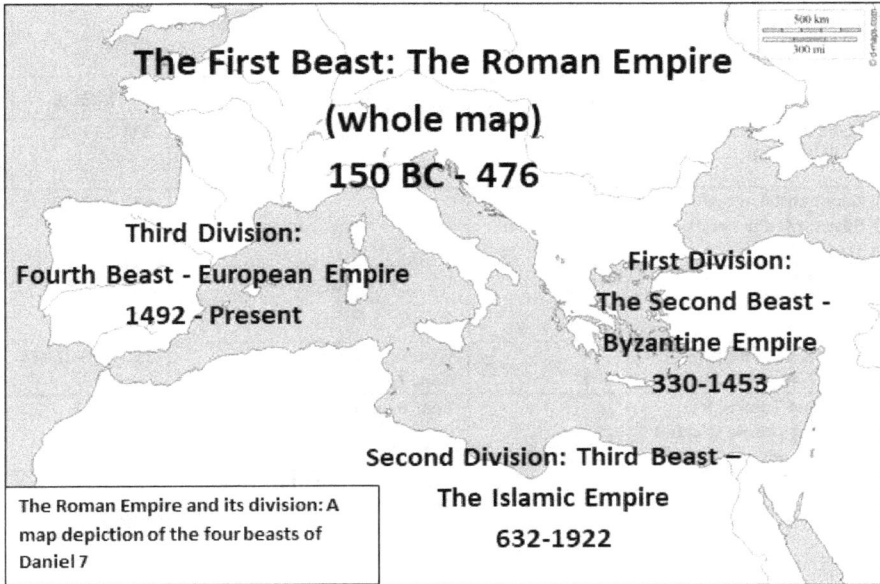

The First Beast: The Roman Empire
(whole map)
150 BC - 476

Third Division:
Fourth Beast - European Empire
1492 - Present

First Division:
The Second Beast -
Byzantine Empire
330-1453

Second Division: Third Beast –
The Islamic Empire
632-1922

The Roman Empire and its division: A map depiction of the four beasts of Daniel 7

If this map could be a clock, the hour hand has traveled full circle by now, and is pointing near midnight, about where Davos, Switzerland is located; where the World Economic Forum holds its annual meetings. Today the world continues under the influence of the West (Europe and its former colonies, to include the U.S., Canada, Australia and others). Although colonization has ceased, this Fourth Beast is still dominating today.

Daniel 2, 8 and 7 Timeline Comparison

Daniel 2	Daniel 8	Daniel 7	Date
Head of Gold: Babylon Dan. 2:37-38			605-539 BC
Chest and Arms of Silver: Medio-Persia Dan. 2:39	Ram: Medio-Persia Dan. 8:3-4, 20		550-330 BC
Belly and Thighs of Bronze: Greece Dan. 2:39	He-Goat: Greece Dan 8:5-8, 21		330-146 BC
Legs of Iron: Rome Dan. 2:40		Winged Lion: Rome Dan. 7:4	150 BC–AD 476
Feet and Toes of Iron and Clay: Rome Divided Dan. 2:41		Bear on one side: Byzantine Empire Dan. 7:5	330-1453
		4-Winged Leopard w/ Four Heads: Islamic Empire Dan. 7:6 Rashidun Caliphate (632-661) Umayyad Caliphate (681-705) Abbasid Dynasty (750-1258) Ottoman Empire (1300-1922)	632-1922
Toes of the Feet of Iron and Clay: Rome Divided Dan. 2:42		10 Horned Beast: European Global Colonization Dan. 7:7, 23-24 10 Colonizing Nations: Spain, Portugal, Netherlands, France, Britain, Sweden, Denmark/Norway, Belgium, Germany, Italy	1492-1999 In 1999 Macau was the last European colony (Portuguese) released from colonialism
		Our Time Now	
		Little Horn King: Dan. 7:8, 24-25	Next
Coming Stone- God's Kingdom: Dan. 2:44-45		God's Coming Kingdom Dan. 7:13-14, 21-22, 26-27	Final/Ending

Chapter 3

Daniel 9: Israel, Jerusalem, and the Broken Timeline

Introduction

Daniel 9:1 In the first year of Darius the son of Ahasuerus, of the seed of the Medes, which was made king over the realm of the Chaldeans;
9:2 In the first year of his reign I Daniel understood by books the number of the years, whereof the word of the LORD came to Jeremiah the prophet, that he would accomplish seventy years in the desolations of Jerusalem.

The time of Babylon had ended. The second kingdom of Daniel 2, the Medes and Persians, had begun their reign, and a now aged Daniel *understood* what he had read from *Jeremiah the prophet*. The *seventy years* of captivity had been accomplished.

Jeremiah 29:10 For thus saith the LORD, That after seventy years be accomplished at Babylon I will visit you, and perform my good word toward you, in causing you to return to this place.

Upon realizing that the time had arrived for the restoration of Israel, Daniel began to seek the Lord in prayer.

Daniel 9:3 And I set my face unto the Lord God, to seek by prayer and supplications, with fasting, and sackcloth, and ashes:

This prayer of Daniel takes up most of chapter 9, and is one of the greatest prayers of the Bible; well worth studying. Our focus is on the answer to this prayer.

The Seventy Weeks

Daniel 9:21 while I was speaking in prayer, the man Gabriel, whom I had seen in the vision at the first, came to me in swift flight at the time of the evening sacrifice.
9:22 He made me understand, speaking with me and saying, "O Daniel, I have now come out to give you insight and understanding. (ESV)

The angel *Gabriel* arrived in answer to Daniel's prayer. Daniel remembered Gabriel from *the vision at the first* (see Dan. 8:16). The following message comes to us from the pen of Daniel, but by the voice of an angel.

Daniel 9:24 Seventy weeks are determined upon thy people and upon thy holy city, to finish the transgression, and to make an end of sins, and to make reconciliation for iniquity, and to bring in everlasting righteousness, and to seal up the vision and prophecy, and to anoint the most Holy.

These *seventy weeks* are weeks of years; seventy years multiplied by seven, or 490 years. Daniel had just read that restoration for his people would arrive after 70 years of captivity in Babylon, according to Jeremiah. Imagine how he must have felt as Gabriel broke the news to him: "not seventy years, Daniel, but seventy years times seven."

To be sure, Jeremiah's prophecy did become a reality and the Jews returned to Jerusalem under Persian rule. This is history. But Daniel was given to know (and share with us) that the Jews returning to the land at that time would not be the end of the matter.

God has a higher purpose for Israel that reaches all the way to the end of this world; because that same purpose reaches all the way back to the beginning, and to the root of the problem – the problem of sin.

This *seventy weeks* of years is a set and determined timeline, and has been placed upon two key components: Daniel's *people* (the Jews), and Jerusalem (*thy holy city*). This is a package deal. It does not say one or the other, but both together. Gabriel also provided a list of accomplishments that would be fulfilled by the end of these *seventy weeks*:

... to finish the transgression, and to make an end of sins, and to make reconciliation for iniquity, and to bring in everlasting righteousness and to seal up the vision and prophecy, and to anoint the most Holy. (9:24)

Looking back to the work of Christ on the cross, we can see that a couple of items on the list have been fulfilled. Some of the others have not. But to be specific, let's have a look at each.

...to finish the transgression. Not complete.

Daniel 9:11 Yea, all Israel have transgressed thy law, even by departing, that they might not obey thy voice; therefore the curse is poured upon us, and the oath that is written in the law of Moses the servant of God, because we have sinned against him.

Israel's *transgression* was not complete at the time of Daniel's prayer. It was not complete when the Jews rejected Jesus as their Messiah. And to this day, Israel still abides in *transgression*. Going by that alone, the *seventy weeks* prophecy is not yet fulfilled.

...to make an end of sins – Not complete.

Sin is still with us. Although Christ has made an end of sin's penalty through His death on the cross, sin has not ended.

1ˢᵗ John 1:9 If we confess our sins, he is faithful and just to forgive us our sins, and to cleanse us from all unrighteousness.

Christians still sin, and the world outside of Christ abides in sin. This still awaits fulfillment.

...to make reconciliation for iniquity – Fulfilled by Christ

2ⁿᵈ Corinthians 5:19 To wit, that God was in Christ, reconciling the world unto himself

Reconciliation has been made. Although this has not been understood or accepted by those who refuse to believe it, it does not negate what was accomplished on the cross.

...to bring in everlasting righteousness – Complete in Christ.

And we may cross this one off the list as well, as the righteousness of God is now available to anyone and everyone who places their faith in Jesus Christ. God's righteousness, which is *everlasting righteousness*, was *brought in* by the work of Jesus Christ on the cross for our behalf.

Romans 3:21 But now the righteousness of God without the law is manifested, being witnessed by the law and the prophets;
3:22 Even the righteousness of God which is by faith of Jesus Christ unto all and upon all them that believe: for there is no difference

...to seal up the vision and prophecy – Uncertain

Because this lacks clarity and can be understood in several ways, we cannot make a final assessment.

...to anoint the most Holy – Uncertain.

Many good biblical expositors and sound Bible commentaries teach that this refers to the *most holy* place in the temple.[xiii] The term, *most holy*, comes from the doubling of the Hebrew word for "holy" (*qodesh*) and is used several times in Scripture for the most holy place in the temple.[xiv] But that same doubling occurs in describing other things as well, such as the sin offering and the trespass offering. Jesus is the fulfillment of both.[xv] He is also our "holy place" before God, who has made us to *sit together in heavenly places in Christ Jesus* (Ephesians 2:6).

While this *anointing* may refer to the most holy place in the temple, it could also be referring to Jesus Christ. He was called Christ (*anointed*) at birth (Luke 2:11). He was *anointed* by God (Luke 4:18). He was also *anointed* by certain women (Matthew 26:7-12; Luke 7:37-46). But since the text here is not specific, and as there is room for disagreement, we cannot be conclusive.

It appears that some of these items have been fulfilled, but not all. Evidently, this prophecy is not yet complete, and we have not reached the end of the *seventy weeks*.

Daniel 9:25-26 – The Broken Timeline

The Two Countdowns

As stated in the Introduction of this book (see *Introduction: A Radical Departure*), this is not the "standard" interpretation, in which the two timelines are combined into one. That was the result of a mistranslation. The early English translators assumed that Jesus, in His first advent, was the fulfillment of this entire *anointed one* passage, and made it read that way. The Hebrew text is not so precise.[xvi] For this reason, our text will be from the Lexham English Bible, which is closer to the original Hebrew.

As we saw in verse 24, Gabriel stated that *seventy weeks* were *determined* upon the Jews and Jerusalem (*thy people and thy holy city*) to accomplish the items we reviewed. In the following verses, Gabriel explains how it all works. Keep in mind that these *weeks* are weeks of years.

Daniel 9:25 And you must know and you must understand that from the time of the going out of the word to restore and build Jerusalem until an anointed one—a leader—will be seven weeks and sixty-two weeks; it will be restored and will be built with streets and a moat, but in a time of oppression.
Dan 9:26 "And after the sixty and two weeks an anointed one shall be cut off, and he shall have nothing, and the people of the coming leader will destroy the city and the sanctuary, and its end will be with the flood and on to the end there shall be war; these desolations are determined.
Dan 9:27 And he will make a strong covenant with the many for one week, ... (LEB)

I called this a broken timeline because this is exactly what it is. It is a set number of 70 weeks of years (9:24), which is then broken down into smaller sets: two countdowns of *weeks* of years (9:25), with a final *week* of years placed at the end (9:27). The two factors upon which this broken timeline is dependent are the people of Israel and the city of Jerusalem: *thy people and thy holy city* (9:24). Both must be together in order for each countdown to begin. The two countdowns also share the same points for activation and termination: *from the time of the going out of the word to restore and build Jerusalem until an anointed one—a leader.*

It is important that we understand that the Hebrew text of verse 25 simply provides two timespans; each beginning with a word or statement to *restore and build Jerusalem,* and each ending with the arrival an *anointed one—a leader.* Although they are presented in a certain order (*seven weeks and sixty-two weeks*), we are not specifically told which would be first. Nor are we told who this *anointed one* or *leader* is. We might also consider that although the Hebrew in verse 25 lacks a conjunction between these two titles (*an anointed one – a leader*), it does not necessarily mean that the *anointed one* has to be the same person as the *leader.* Both titles are used again in verse 26, and distinguishes the *anointed one* from the *coming leader,* obviously referring to two different people. And so we have two countdowns; two separate acts of sending out the word to restore and build Jerusalem that end with two different *leaders.*

The first *Anointed One* was Jesus Christ. He arrived at the end of the *sixty-two weeks* countdown, and was *cut off.* The other will be *the coming leader.*

The Sixty-Two Weeks: The Anointed One

Daniel 9:26 "And after the sixty and two weeks an anointed one shall be cut off, …" (LEB)

There is the only one known statement, or *word* to *restore and build Jerusalem* that fits with the *sixty-two weeks* portion of the prophecy. It is found in Nehemiah 2:1-8. Under Persian rule, the Jews and Jerusalem were united again after the Babylonian captivity, and had already built their temple. In verses 5 and 6, Nehemiah received permission from the king of Persia to build and restore Jerusalem.

Nehemiah 2:5 And I said unto the king: 'If it please the king, and if thy servant have found favour in thy sight, that thou wouldest send me unto Judah, unto the city of my fathers' sepulchres, that I may build it.'
2:6 And the king said unto me, the queen also sitting by him: 'For how long shall thy journey be? and when wilt thou return?' So it pleased the king to send me; and I set him a time.

The king is Artaxerxes I, who reigned from around 465 to 424 BC (approximate). It was twenty years into his reign (Neh. 2:1) that his word of permission began the countdown placing the *sixty-two weeks* portion (434 years) of the 70 week prophecy well within range of the first advent of Jesus Christ.[xvii]

The angels declared Him "Christ" (anointed) at His birth (Luke 2:11). Jesus is the *Anointed One* who was also *cut off* when He was crucified (Dan. 9:26). Note that Gabriel did not say how long *after* the 62 weeks (of years) that *an anointed one* would be *cut off*. He merely stated that it would happen *after* the 62 weeks.

And so it was a little over thirty years *after* His birth that Jesus was crucified. The added detail, *"and he shall have nothing"* (v. 26, LEB) may be read to understand that this *Anointed One* did not receive what was due Him (which would have been His kingdom at that time) because His people did not receive Him (John 1:11). They cut Him off. The King James rendering is different. It states that He was *"cut off, but not for Himself"*. Christ died on the cross, not for Himself but for the sins of the world, so that we might have everlasting life by believing in Him (John 20:31). Both renderings are valid.

... and the people of the prince that shall come shall destroy the city and the sanctuary; Daniel 9:26 (KJV)

Jerusalem was destroyed in AD 70 by the Roman armies (*the people of the prince that shall come*). Since this also happened *after* the *threescore and two weeks*, we can say that this part of the prophecy has been fulfilled.

The Jews and the *holy city* have since been separated for about 2,000 years, setting aside the next countdown (the *seven weeks*, or 49 years) for a later time.

The Seven Weeks: The Coming Prince

Daniel 9:25 And you must know and you must understand that from the time of the going out of the word to restore and build Jerusalem until an anointed one—a leader—will be seven weeks... (LEB)

With the fall of Jerusalem in AD 70, the Jews (*thy people*) and Jerusalem (*thy holy city*) were no longer together. But in 1948 Israel became a nation again, and the Jews have been returning to their land. In 1950, the Israeli parliament declared Jerusalem the capital of Israel and major government offices were moved there.[xviii] But at that time the city was divided, with Jordan in control of the eastern part, which includes the original site of ancient Jerusalem where Temple Mount is also located.

In 1967, as a result of the Six Day War, Israel regained all of Jerusalem once again. The year 1967 marks the reconnection of the Jews (*thy people*) with Jerusalem (*thy holy city*). On July 30, 1980, Israel again declared Jerusalem its capital.[xix]

And so we have a few things to consider. Has there been any kind of statement put forth about the rebuilding or restoring of Jerusalem since 1967? It may be that we are already living within the final *seven weeks* (49 years). Presently, the UN has placed the Old City on its World Heritage list to protect it as is, a possible hindrance to Israel for building or adding anything in that locality.[xx] But this does not necessarily mean that Israel is abiding by UN directives.

On another front, we should also recall that at the end of the *sixty-two weeks*, the *Anointed One*, Jesus Christ, arrived as a newborn baby. He still had another thirty years to grow up and begin His ministry before being *cut off*. Likewise, we may be looking to a birth event here as well.

So for example, if in 1967 some kind of statement was put forth to restore Jerusalem, this coming prince may have been born sometime around 2016 and will be thirty years old by 2046. Or if it was July 1980 or thereabouts, when Jerusalem was declared the capital, he might be born around 2029, and would turn 30 by 2059. But this is merely one consideration.

Gabriel's prophecy does not specify physical birth. It specifies an *anointed one*, and a *coming leader.* Luke 2:11 tells us that Jesus was recognized as Christ (*Anointed*) at His birth. This other fellow will be recognized as a *leader*. There is no requirement that recognition for this *coming leader* take place at his birth. Recognition, or *anointing*, or coronation, or whatever form in which it comes can occur at any given point in one's life.

Although we do not know all the details, we are certainly in the ballpark for this person's arrival. He is coming, and he may be alive today. But we must also recognize that we are cruising in uncharted waters.

Daniel 9:27: The Final Week

Daniel 9:27 And he shall confirm the covenant with many for one week: and in the midst of the week he shall cause the sacrifice and the oblation to cease, and for the overspreading of abominations he shall make it desolate, even until the consummation, and that determined shall be poured upon the desolate. (KJV)

And he shall confirm the covenant with many for one week: a week of years. This is the last seven years, and it will come as a seven year *covenant*. The word *covenant*, as translated from the original Hebrew (בְּרִית, *berîyth*), also means *alliance*, or *treaty;* and has been used this way a few times in Scripture.[xxi] It may be that this *covenant* will be similar to the Middle East peace treaties that have been attempted in recent years.[xxii] Or, the reference of *many* (or *the many* – LITV, LEB) may indicate a covenant between the world leader with the global community (the *many* as opposed to *the few* Matthew 7:13-14). Whatever form it comes in, *alliance*, *covenant* or *treaty*, we are given to know that it will be sold as a seven year event.

The Abomination of Desolation

In the midst of the week (three and a half years), it says that *he shall cause the sacrifice and the oblation* will *cease*. It does not say how or why he does this. But in order for something to *cease*, it must have already been ongoing by this time. Sacrifice and offering implies an existing temple. At the time of this writing, there is no temple in Jerusalem. But there will be.[xxiii]

The next phrase in the verse is somewhat unclear:

...and for the overspreading of abominations he shall make it desolate, - 9:27

Because of the obscurity of the Hebrew text here, this phrase has been variously translated by the scholars. Here are a few examples of the same phrase from some of the other English Bibles:

And on the wing of abominations shall come one who makes desolate (ESV)

...upon the wing of detestable things shall be that which causeth appalment (JPS)

...by the wing of abominations he is making desolate (LSV)

And on a corner of the altar will be abominations that desolate, (LITV)

Even the professional translators have a difficult time with this one. But taking a look at some of the Hebrew words used here, alongside what other Scriptures have to say in connection with the same words, we might be able to shed some light on what this phrase is saying. We'll work from the King James.

...and for the overspreading of abominations he shall make it desolate. (KJV)

The first words of the phrase, *and for*, come from the Hebrew, עַל (or *'al*), which carries a meaning of "placement in relation to something else," as in *upon, adjoining, against, between*, etc.,[xxiv] and this is evident in some of the translations above.

The word used for *overspreading*, is from כָּנָף, (or *kânâph*) and actually means wing.[xxv] It is the same word used for the wings of the cherubim (winged angels) in both the tabernacle and the temple (Exodus 25:18-20; 2nd Chron. 5:7-8). It makes sense that *wing*, or wings, is accurate here, since the verse references *the sacrifice and the oblation*, which implies the existence of the temple. It is likely that we are being told about something or someone (the Hebrew does not specify) inside the temple.

Within the temple is an inner room that's called the *oracle*, or *inner sanctuary* (1st Kings 6:19-23). It is also known as the *Holy of holies*. Inside that room are two golden cherubim with outstretched wings. The mention of a *wing* (or wings), and of something, or someone in close proximity, gives the location of whatever or whoever is in there. Scripture tells us that it (or he) will be an *abomination*; and will be the cause of *desolation*. But we really don't have to be unclear. Jesus plainly stated that this abomination will be inside the temple, in the holy place.

Matthew 24:15 When ye therefore shall see the abomination of desolation, spoken of by Daniel the prophet, stand in the holy place, (whoso readeth, let him understand:) 24:16 Then let them which be in Judaea flee into the mountains:

24:21 For then shall be great tribulation, such as was not since the beginning of the world to this time, no, nor ever shall be.

This *abomination of desolation* standing *in the holy place* marks the beginning of the coming *great tribulation*. Taking place *in the midst of the week*, this begins the final three and a half years that will complete the *seventy weeks* prophecy of Daniel 9.

Conclusion

As with the *little horn* king of Daniel 7, we are again in uncharted waters with this *prince that shall come* and his seven year *covenant*. Is this *prince* the same person as the *little horn* king? Or are they separate entities? We are told in the book of Revelation that there will be two leaders, the beast and the false prophet (Rev. 16:13; 20:10). Again, we are in unfamiliar territory and cannot conclude based on our partial knowledge at this time. But neither can we discount the information that we do have.

The recent return of the Jews to Israel, and more recently, Israel's gaining of all of Jerusalem in 1967 places us in a position for the final *seven weeks* countdown. Has there been any command or statement to *restore and build Jerusalem* in recent years? There may have been several plans put forth for restoration or modernization, or for rebuilding the Old City. And if this is the case, how may we know which one might be the "switch" that activates the countdown to this *coming leader*?

Presently, there is no temple in Jerusalem. There are no sacrifices or offerings taking place. No one has made a seven year covenant or agreement yet. These things are coming, and we should be watchful. We missed rightly identifying the four beasts of Daniel 7 over the last two thousand years as they were passing over us. We might miss these things as well when they are upon us. We need to pray for revelation and discernment.

Daniel 2, 7 and Daniel 9 Timeline Comparison

Daniel 2, and 7: Gentile Nations	Daniel 9: Jews and Jerusalem
Babylonian Empire 605-539 BC (Head of Gold Dan. 2:37-38)	Babylonian captivity
Medio-Persian Empire: 550-330 BC (Chest and Arms of Silver Dan.2:39 & Ram of Dan.8:20)	Babylonian Captivity Ends (Jeremiah 29:10; Daniel 9:2) 538 BC
	Permission to Rebuild Jerusalem by Artaxerxes I (465-424 BC) 70 Weeks Prophecy Begins: First 62 Weeks (434 Years) to an anointed one. Fulfillment will be Jesus Christ.
Greek Empire: 330 BC-146 BC (Belly and thighs of Bronze - Dan. 2:39 & Male Goat of Daniel 8:21)	
Roman Empire: 150 BC – AD 476 (Legs of Iron Dan. 2:40 & Winged Lion – Dan. 7:4)	The Anointed One: 62 weeks fulfilled by the birth of Jesus (4-7 BC, approximate). Validated by the magi (Mat. 2:1-12). AD 27 (approximate) - Messiah cut off Jesus is crucified. (Dan. 9:26) AD 70 - Jerusalem Destroyed by Roman armies. Jews and Jerusalem separated. (Dan. 9:26)
Byzantine Empire: 330 - 1453 (Iron and Clay -Divided Roman Empire Dan. 2:41 & Bear on one side– Daniel 7:5)	
Islamic Empire: 632-1922 (Iron and Clay – Divided Roman Empire Dan. 2:41 & 4-Winged Leopard with 4 Heads – Daniel 7:6)	
European Global Conquest and Colonization: 1492-1937 (colonization ceases) (10 Toes of Iron and Clay -Divided Roman Empire of Dan. 2:42 & 10-Horned Beast of Daniel 7:7)	1948 – Israel becomes a nation again – Ongoing war with surrounding nations. 1967 – Six Day War - Jews and Jerusalem reunited 1980 – Israel makes Jerusalem its capital
1999 – Macau is the last European colony (Portuguese) released from colonialism – ending the 10-Horns period of the Fourth Beast of Daniel 7. Our Time Now	Our Time Now
Uncharted Territory:	Uncharted Territory:
Coming "Little Horn" King (Final stage of the fourth beast of Daniel 7 - Daniel 7:8, 24-25)	Command to rebuild Jerusalem to begin the 7 Weeks/49 years until the coming prince (not Jesus).- Dan. 9:25-26 Final Week: 7-year covenant. Halfway point –Sacrifice and Offering stops Abomination of Desolation. (Daniel 9:27)
Kingdom of God Arrives and destroys kingdoms of this world (Daniel 2:44-45, 7:13-14; 26-27)	Consummation (Dan. 9:27)

Chapter 4

The New Testament

Introduction

The book of Daniel carried us across the ages through imagery that foretold a succession of empires that end with the arrival of God's kingdom. In Daniel 9, we read about the two timelines placed upon the Jews and Jerusalem, and saw that one of them has already been played out; fulfilled to the letter at the first advent of Jesus Christ.

Looking back into history, we find that the prophecies of Daniel are largely fulfilled. Nearly every kingdom (or beast) has come and gone since Daniel was written. And today we live in a world that has been colonized by the European nations – the 10 horns of that fourth and final beast (Dan. 7:23-24). Although the colonizing has ceased and the colonies released, the world today continues under the dominating influence of the same Western powers; the same beast, the same iron and clay of Daniel 2. But there is one more leader yet to come, that final horn. Today, Israel is again a nation on the map after nearly 2,000 years, and Jerusalem is its capital; enabling the timer for the second countdown to the *coming prince* of Daniel 9, who will not be Jesus Christ.

The New Testament also contains some identifiers to help us understand *when we are* today in relation to His coming. The first advent of Jesus Christ ushered the world into its last days, reaching its first climax at His death, burial, resurrection and ascension. Today we live in the age of Grace, and of the Good News of reconciliation with God by what Christ accomplished on the cross. And the writers of our New Testament have given us additional information of what to expect as that Day of His return approaches.

Matthew 24: The Olivet Discourse

Matthew 24:3 And as he sat upon the mount of Olives, the disciples came unto him privately, saying, Tell us, when shall these things be? and what shall be the sign of thy coming, and of the end of the world?

It's known as the Olivet Discourse because of the location. And this is appropriate; because when Jesus returns, this is where He will stand:

Zechariah 14:3 Then shall the LORD go forth, and fight against those nations, as when he fought in the day of battle.
14:4 And his feet shall stand in that day upon the mount of Olives, which is before Jerusalem on the east, and the mount of Olives shall cleave in the midst thereof toward the east and toward the west, and there shall be a very great valley; and half of the mountain shall remove toward the north, and half of it toward the south.

It was here, on that same Mount of Olives, from which He also ascended up into the cloud (Acts 1:9-11), that Jesus sat down two thousand years ago and began to tell His disciples of things to come, before He comes. Let's see what He says.

Take Heed

Matthew 24:4 And Jesus answered and said unto them, Take heed that no man deceive you.
24:5 For many shall come in my name, saying, I am Christ; and shall deceive many.

The first words out of His mouth were words of warning against deception, and that deception has everything to do with Him! *Many* will come in His name; and *many* have. *Many* will. And *many* have been and will continue to be deceived.

The saying, *I am Christ,* as it appears in this passage has traditionally been understood to mean that *many* would come and claim to be *Christ*, or the Messiah. And while some have done this from time to time, we do not find *many* people in history who actually claimed to be Christ.[xxvi]

Because of this problem, some Bible commentaries and Bible teachers say that Jesus is referring to the distant future, to the time of the tribulation and antichrist.[xxvii] And this will happen, as Jesus will tell us down in verse 24. But here at the outset of his discourse, it is apparent that Jesus is warning His disciples of a very imminent deception. And as we will see, it happened.

One of the problems that we have in reading is that we don't hear the voice of the speaker. There is no inflection or stress on certain words that might communicate meaning more precisely. This is one reason that written communication is often misunderstood. With that in mind, if we read this phrase a little differently, we'll find that it makes more sense to reality and resonates with history as we know it. It also helps to be mindful of the context of that time in relation to what Jesus said.

When Jesus walked the earth in human flesh, not many believed that He was the Christ (the Messiah). He had His disciples, which amounted to about 120 in the upper room according to the book of Acts (Acts 1:15). But let's back up to when Jesus asked His disciples what *other* people believed about Him. What did *they* say?

Matthew 16:14 And they said, Some say that thou art John the Baptist: some, Elias; and others, Jeremias, or one of the prophets.

People were divided as to who Jesus was. There was no consensus or agreement about His identity during His earthly ministry. But here in Matthew 24:5, Jesus is saying that very soon, many *will* confess that He is Christ, but will be *deceivers*. When we read it with that in mind, the statement takes on a different meaning.

The *"I"* of 24:5 is probably *not* the deceivers saying that *they* are Christ. It more likely means that deceivers will come and acknowledge that *Jesus* is Christ. The word, *"saying"*, in the original Greek, also carries a meaning of *affirming*. The verse could also be read like this:

"For many shall come in my name, *affirming* I am Christ."[xxviii]

When we read it that way, the light comes on. And we can easily see the *many* throughout the ages following these deceivers who readily agree that Jesus is the Christ, all the way back to the apostolic age: right into legalism (Galatians); right into Gnosticism and other false teachings (Colossians, 2nd Corinthians, 1st John); into idolatry and persecuting real Christians; into war and the crusades (Middle Ages); into the cults; and into padding the pockets of the televangelists of our own time. *Many* have acknowledged that Jesus is Christ, and have deceived *many*.

The Beginning of Sorrows

Matthew 24:6 And ye shall hear of wars and rumours of wars: see that ye be not troubled: for all these things must come to pass, but the end is not yet.
24:7 For nation shall rise against nation, and kingdom against kingdom: and there shall be famines, and pestilences, and earthquakes, in divers places.

In reading these words, it becomes obvious that Jesus is moving beyond the lifetimes of His hearers. He knew His words would be put into writing. He knew that you would be reading this right now. One of the ways of God throughout Scripture is that He often speaks beyond His immediate audience.[xxix] The natural rendering of our text indicates a long time-span, and Jesus is speaking to us today through His written Word.

Looking back into history, we see that war is part of the heritage of humanity. There seems to be no end to it (*but the end is not yet*). Famines and plagues have come and gone, and will return to visit again. Earthquakes and natural disasters have continued to this day. This is the world we know. This is normal for us. But think about this for a moment. In the day when Jesus walked the earth and the kingdom of God was at hand, how different our world might have been had Israel accepted her Messiah in her day of visitation.[xxx]

Jesus said that all these things were coming. Jerusalem would not be the only city to be leveled, in the greater scheme of things. This whole world has suffered these two-thousand years as a direct result of Israel's rejection of her Messiah. But even this has its purpose in the will of God. Suffering and grace go hand in hand. It happened on the cross, and it's still happening today.

Matthew 24:8 All these are the beginning of sorrows.

The word, *sorrows*, in the original Greek, means *birth pangs.*[xxxi] Descriptive of a woman in her pregnancy, birth pangs increase in frequency and intensity until that final throe, when the child is born. And this world, with all its pain and anguish, ebbing and flowing like a woman in labor, is headed toward that final climax; the birth of the new creation. Here's what it says in Romans:

Romans 8:22 For we know that the whole creation has been groaning together in the pains of childbirth until now. (ESV)

Not so very long ago, the last global war ended with a grim foreboding; an all too real dread of what lay on the horizon. What happened in 1945 to Hiroshima and Nagasaki shook the world. If compared to a woman in travail, she might easily have shouted, "This is it! It's coming!"

That wasn't the end; but the world at that time took note, and the churches were full. We are almost there, and He is coming.

Christian Persecution

Matthew 24:9 Then shall they deliver you up to be afflicted, and shall kill you: and ye shall be hated of all nations for my name's sake.

The word, *then*, does not necessarily mean, *after this. Then* also means, *at that time*, or at the same time these other things are occurring. The persecutions were initiated by the Jews in the first century who saw Christianity as a threat to Judaism (Acts 8:1). After that it was the Romans, and then it spread throughout the world, wherever the gospel is preached.

The Scandalizing

Matthew 24:10 And then shall many be offended, and shall betray one another, and shall hate one another.

We cannot pass the word, *offended*, without some further explanation. In our time, the name of Jesus has often been withheld or suppressed to avoid "offending" someone. But the original Greek word used here is *skandalizo*, and can be used in several ways.

The definition below is taken from <u>Thayer's Greek Lexicon of the New Testament</u>, *e-Sword* edition (download)[xxxii]:

skandalizō (σκανδαλίζω)

Thayer Definition:

1) to put a stumbling block or impediment in the way, upon which another may trip and fall, metaphorically to offend

1a) to entice to sin

1b) to cause a person to begin to distrust and desert one whom he ought to trust and obey

1b1) to cause to fall away

1b2) to be offended in one, i.e. to see in another what I disapprove of and what hinders me from acknowledging his authority

1b3) to cause one to judge unfavourably or unjustly of another

Evidently, the word, *scandalize*, is far more encompassing than the word, *offended*. It seems that Jesus knew what He was saying as He spoke to, and throughout the generations to come. The word in its most common form today means something similar to *offended*,[xxxiii] and many have truly been *offended* by more things than the name of Jesus. Particularly offensive in our times is much of what is presented in today's common media: television, movies, the news, internet, etc. And interestingly on that note, a trend has developed in which by constant exposure, things once considered scandalous have become cultural norms, causing many to *stumble* and to be *led into sin*. In that sense, many have truly been *scandalized*.

Going by Thayer's definition 1b1) above, other English translations (NASB, ISV, EMTV, and others) have chosen to use *fall away* (or *turn away*) rather than the word, *offended*, in their texts. The following is from the English Standard Version:

Matthew 24:10 And then many will fall away and betray one another and hate one another. (ESV)

This is significant. Although the Greek word used here is not the same as the one we will be examining in 2nd Thessalonians 2:3 (*The Apostasy*), the meaning is the same. The fact that Jesus places this *falling away* here in His order of events is no coincidence. We will visit this again.

According to Thayer's definition 1b3) above, to *scandalize* also means something that is done purposely to destroy one's character – to *scandalize* someone. For example, when people in positions of power and influence do not like a particular message, but cannot refute it, they normally *scandalize* the messenger.

74

Today we call it "character assassination". It's a time-tested and proven method of intimidation that suppresses the message by turning people away from the messenger; normally by spreading false information or linking them with anything socially unacceptable. It's the same tactic the scribes and Pharisees used for the purpose of suppressing the message of Jesus. And if you have been paying attention, it is also done to the Bible in our own time.

Today we see it working in politics and in the news media. New words have been coined for this purpose, and we watched as new "phobias" have been added to our vocabulary and attached to people who don't approve of particular kinds of sinful activity. And to speak out against certain sins may easily have one publicly smeared for "hate speech." *Scandalizing* comes in many forms.

Mass Deception

Matthew 24:11 And many false prophets shall rise, and shall deceive many.

Jesus had already said that many would come *in His name* in order to *deceive many* (v. 5). Here, He does not attach the *false prophets* and their deception to Himself as He did in verse 5. Not all false prophets come in the name of Jesus. The religions of this world, for example, do not acknowledge Jesus Christ, and they attract *many* followers. But have you considered that not all false prophets are religious? In the West, we have our prophets of secular humanism. It's what they profess.

The apostle John provides a simple identifier for recognizing these *false prophets*. If they don't confess Jesus, they're not from God.

1st John 4:1 Beloved, do not believe every spirit, but test the spirits to see whether they are from God, for many false prophets have gone out into the world.
4:2 By this you know the Spirit of God: every spirit that confesses that Jesus Christ has come in the flesh is from God,
4:3 and every spirit that does not confess Jesus is not from God. This is the spirit of the antichrist, which you heard was coming and now is in the world already. (ESV)

The *false prophets* in John's day were known as Gnostics. While they proclaimed that Jesus was Christ (as Jesus had already forewarned –Mat. 24:5), they denied that He had *come in the flesh*. And they deceived *many*. Throughout history, there have been *many* false prophets, both inside and outside the church. And *many* have been and continue to be *deceived*.

Today we hear their voices in the documentaries about nature and science, proclaiming their message of "evolution." We find them among the anchor men and women on network news. They are found in our schools and colleges teaching our children. They come in the form of talk show hosts and entertainers. These are the prophets of secularism and sin. We identify them by what comes out of their mouths. They are not from God, neither is their message from God. There are *many* of them, and their purpose (whether they themselves are aware of it or not) is to *deceive many*. And Jesus already told us to *take heed*.

John told us how to spot the false prophets. The Psalmist tells us how to avoid their trap.

One simple way to help us *take heed* is to read and memorize the first words of Psalm 1, and put them into practice.

Psalm 1:1 Blessed is the man that walketh not in the counsel of the ungodly, nor standeth in the way of sinners, nor sitteth in the seat of the scornful.

The way of blessing, according to this verse, is to avoid *ungodly counsel*. Any *counsel*, advice, or teaching that is contrary to God's Word is *ungodly* by definition. For example, Scripture tells us that the entire human race descended from Adam and Eve, who are direct creations of God. The gospel of Luke complements Scripture by tracing the human side of Christ's genealogy all the way back to Adam, who was created by God from the dust of the earth.

The teaching that humans naturally evolved from lower life forms is therefore an *ungodly* teaching by definition; and those who proclaim this message of natural selection (as opposed to Divine creation) are, in effect, making themselves into antichrists and modern false prophets. Likewise, those who proclaim and support activities that are sinful according to Scripture are also speaking contrary to the Word of God, and can also be categorized along with the *false prophets* and *antichrists*.

Jesus said that *many* would be deceived. Take a look around. Does the evidence match what Jesus said? Of course it does.

Abounding Iniquity

Matthew 24:12 And because iniquity shall abound, the love of many shall wax cold.
24:13 But he that shall endure unto the end, the same shall be saved.

The Greek word for *love* in this passage is *agape*. It is the same word found in John 3:16; that kind of *love* demonstrated by Christ on the cross. Humanity has no claim to this kind of love outside of His love for us first (1st John 4:19), and our receiving it. So when Jesus says to *endure*, He isn't speaking of people who don't know Him. In fact, this abounding *iniquity* by those who know not Christ is a primary reason that God's people have to *endure*.

Iniquity abounds. It always has. The prophets of the Old Testament lamented the *abounding iniquity* of their times. One example should suffice. Listen to the words of Habakkuk:

Habakkuk 1:2 O LORD, how long shall I cry, and thou wilt not hear! even cry out unto thee of violence, and thou wilt not save! 1:3 Why dost thou shew me iniquity, and cause me to behold grievance? for spoiling and violence are before me: and there are that raise up strife and contention. 1:4 Therefore the law is slacked, and judgment doth never go forth: for the wicked doth compass about the righteous; therefore wrong judgment proceedeth.

And if you care to do the research, some of the most horrible times come right out of the history of the church; Christians (that's what they called themselves) persecuting Christians, burning them alive, as Christians stood by, unable to do anything about it.[xxxiv]

Iniquity abounded in the church throughout the middle ages. On one hand there were real Christians seeking a close relationship with the Father through the Son by His Spirit. On the other side there were "religious" people who called themselves by that same name, many holding high offices inside and outside the church, committing all kinds of abominations, and persecuting those who got out of line. Not much different from today - the only things that have changed are the names and titles.

Iniquity truly abounds. And the unsaved (or *them that perish* – 1 Cor. 1:18) have always been the primary practitioners and supporters of it: fornication (all varieties of sexual activity outside of marriage), murder (including abortion as a tragedy of convenience, or euthanasia), theft (to include legal theft through taxation, or providing deceptive information to receive financial aid or benefits), and *scandalizing* those who disapprove of such things are merely a few examples of *abounding iniquity*.

We have seen *iniquity* abound in government and in the courts. We see it on the mainstream media by television and internet. And we've seen it in the churches. We have watched as it is has been and continues to be promoted and protected as some new freedom, or masqueraded with minority status on the same level as race or skin color. Nor have we been blind as it has been minimized by those in power who try to hide it from the public. It is frustrating to watch as morals and values are trampled underfoot as sin is paraded in triumph as some new kind of social justice, while God's people are purposely *scandalized* with terms of hate and intolerance; and that in a society that once held to biblical values.

What makes it all the more difficult is that as one draws closer to God by His process of sanctification into His likeness, and begins to view the activities of this world more in line with the way God sees them, it doesn't help that everyone, including friends and family, appears to be moving rapidly in the opposite direction. We are grieved by it. And yet, we are told to *endure*.

And this does not even begin to touch the most abhorrent atrocities Christians face all over the world through persecution. To this very day, villages are burned, women and girls of all ages are raped and murdered, small children are chopped to pieces in front of their mothers.[xxxv] It is truly amazing that love could possibly endure under the pressures of that level of cruelty. And yet, real Christians still forgive, and love their enemies; demonstrating that same love exemplified by Jesus Christ on the cross.

A good study of 1st John (particularly chapters 3-5), and put into practice, might be in order for these troubling times. We need to guard our hearts, so that our love (our *agape* love) does not grow cold. We are to *endure unto the end,* be it the end of this age, or the end of our lives.

1ˢᵗ John 4:16 And we have known and believed the love that God hath to us. God is love; and he that dwelleth in love dwelleth in God, and God in him.
4:17 Herein is our love made perfect, that we may have boldness in the day of judgment: because as he is, so are we in this world.

This Gospel of the Kingdom

Matthew 24:14 And this gospel of the kingdom shall be preached in all the world for a witness unto all nations; and then shall the end come.^{xxxvi}

Jesus is specific when He says *this gospel of the kingdom;* not to be confused with the gospel of salvation through His death, burial and resurrection. Jesus had not yet gone to the cross, and it was still that same *gospel of the kingdom* that both He and John the Baptist proclaimed to the Jews that He is referring to here. The Jews had the Scriptures. They knew the prophecies. They understood that God would one day establish His kingdom on earth. They knew that the LORD would reign in Jerusalem. Both John and Jesus told them to get ready, because the kingdom of heaven was at hand. And yet, both were rejected and killed by their people.

But Jesus did not stay dead.

The death, burial and resurrection of Jesus Christ brought the gospel of salvation, because it was on the cross that Jesus became the sacrifice for the sins of the whole world (1st John 2:2). From that time to our time, the gospel of salvation has been proclaimed to the nations; and what was once restricted to Israel now belongs to the disciples of Jesus Christ in every nation, tongue and tribe.

Alongside Israel, we too now have the prophecies. We too now understand that God will establish His kingdom on earth. We too now know that He will reign in Jerusalem. But unlike Israel, who rejected their Messiah, we know who will sit on the throne, and that Person is Jesus Christ.

As it was in Israel two thousand years ago, so it is now all over the earth. For wherever the gospel of salvation is proclaimed, *this gospel of the kingdom* is sure to follow. *And then the end will come.*

Everything that Jesus said in this prophecy has been fulfilled throughout history down to our own time. And aside from the *gospel of the kingdom* preached to the nations, all of it is negative. Like *birth pangs*, these things have also increased in frequency and intensity. The twentieth century has seen two global wars. It has seen genocide and mass executions on a scale unparalleled by any other time in known history.[xxxvii]

The twenty-first century opened with the horrific attack on the World Trade Center by Al-Qaeda, leading to war and devastation in Afghanistan, and war in Iraq. More recently, the Taliban has retaken Afghanistan, and Russia has invaded the Ukraine. A group called Hamas invaded Israel from Gaza, butchering families in their homes and started another war. Even as I write this, Iran has just fired missiles at Israel. All the while, China has been actively working at taking over the South China Sea, claiming islands that belong to other nations. Wars have not ended. The *birth pangs* continue.

Hurricanes, tornadoes, and earthquakes (some resulting in devastating tsunamis) seem to have noticeably increased, with world leaders today blaming human induced climate change as the cause. The *birth pangs* haven't stopped.

What Jesus mentions next has not yet happened. Once again, we are sailing into uncharted waters – but for how long?

The Great Tribulation

Matthew 24:15 When ye therefore shall see the abomination of desolation, spoken of by Daniel the prophet, stand in the holy place, (whoso readeth, let him understand:)

In introducing this *abomination of desolation*, Jesus points back to *Daniel the prophet.* We saw this in Daniel 9:26-27. The *prince that shall come* will make a seven year covenant, but in the middle of those seven years, he will somehow cause the sacrifice and offering to cease. It is then that this *abomination of desolation* will appear in the temple. Here in Matthew 24:15, Jesus says that it (or he) will *stand in the holy place.* Once this *abomination* is seen in the temple, the Great Tribulation has begun.

Matthew 24:16 Then let them which be in Judaea flee into the mountains: 24:17 Let him which is on the housetop not come down to take anything out of his house: 24:18 Neither let him which is in the field return back to take his clothes.
24:19 And woe unto them that are with child, and to them that give suck in those days! 24:20 But pray ye that your flight be not in the winter, neither on the sabbath day: 24:21 For then shall be great tribulation, such as was not since the beginning of the world to this time, no, nor ever shall be.

Then let them which be in Judaea flee. This will not be the time to be living in Israel. Jesus is addressing Jews here. But this would likely include anyone who sympathizes with them, as well as Christians living in Judea at that time. In short, Christ's message to the people in Judea during this time is to *run, hide,* and *don't go back*; with a special *woe* for women with children.

He says that this will be a time, the likes of which the world has never seen, nor ever will see again. Jesus also said that this coming time will be so devastating that without some kind of supernatural intervention, all life would end:

Matthew 24:22 And except those days should be shortened, there should no flesh be saved: but for the elect's sake those days shall be shortened.

Days during the tribulation will be shortened – *for the elect's sake.* We find a similar reference to *shortened days* in the book of Revelation.

Revelation 8:12 And the fourth angel sounded, and the third part of the sun was smitten, and the third part of the moon, and the third part of the stars; so as the third part of them was darkened, and the day shone not for a third part of it, and the night likewise.

One third of a day will be gone. Days will be shortened to about 16 hours. It may be that the earth's rotation will have a catastrophic increase in speed – *for the elect's sake.* That's you and me, if your faith is in Jesus Christ. We are the elect.

Colossians 3:12 Put on therefore, as God's elect, holy and beloved, a heart of compassion, kindness, lowliness, meekness, longsuffering;
3:13 forbearing one another, and forgiving each other, if any man have a complaint against any; even as the Lord forgave you, so also do ye: (ASV)

Don't let your love grow cold.

False Messiahs, False Signs

Matthew 24:23 "At that time if anyone should say to you, 'Behold, here is the Christ,' or 'Here he is,' do not believe him!
24:24 For false messiahs and false prophets will appear, and will produce great signs and wonders in order to deceive, if possible, even the elect.
24:25 Behold, I have told you ahead of time!
24:26 Therefore if they say to you, 'Behold, he is in the wilderness,' do not go out, or 'Behold, he is in the inner rooms,' do not believe it! (LEB)

At that time: It will be no secret by the time of the tribulation that Christ's coming will be close at hand. Anticipation among God's people will run high, and Satan will know that his time is short (Rev. 12:12). The purpose of the *false messiahs and false prophets* is to *deceive*. Don't be taken by surprise when they produce *signs and wonders.* Most of us know people who are easily amazed (and deceived) by the *signs and wonders* of today's televangelists. And they will likely be very susceptible to this coming deception (perhaps these things *are* that coming deception). But Jesus already warned us beforehand that this is what these deceivers are going to do. And if it is at all possible, they will deceive *even the elect!*[xxxviii] Be on your guard!

Jesus warns us to not believe these people, nor go looking for Him in the places where they tell us to look. He adds, *Behold, I have told you ahead of time!* We know in advance that they will do these things. No matter how excited you are, or how much you want to see Him, do NOT believe these people; not even if they are your pastors or the ones who led you to Christ. Do NOT go to the places where they say He is. Because when He comes, everybody is going to see it. It will be no secret.

Matthew 24:27 For just as the lightning comes from the east and flashes to the west, so the coming of the Son of Man will be. (LEB)

Although we have ventured into uncharted territory, I thought it good to include this portion of Scripture for the sake of those who will be here when these times arrive; and particularly the warning to avoid the trap of looking for Jesus where He is not.

Luke 21: The Times of the Gentiles

Luke 21:20 And when ye shall see Jerusalem compassed with armies, then know that the desolation thereof is nigh.
21:21 Then let them which are in Judaea flee to the mountains; and let them which are in the midst of it depart out; and let not them that are in the countries enter thereinto.
21:22 For these be the days of vengeance, that all things which are written may be fulfilled.
21:23 But woe unto them that are with child, and to them that give suck, in those days! for there shall be great distress in the land, and wrath upon this people.
21:24 And they shall fall by the edge of the sword, and shall be led away captive into all nations: and Jerusalem shall be trodden down of the Gentiles, until the times of the Gentiles be fulfilled.

This is Christ's prophecy about the destruction of Jerusalem, which was fulfilled in AD 70. It is similar to Matthew 24, with a few exceptions. Matthew 24 makes no mention of *Jerusalem encompassed with armies* (v. 20). And here, there is no mention of an abomination of desolation. Unlike the great tribulation, which will involve the whole world, and will be worse than anything the world has ever seen or will ever see again, the *great distress* here is local, *in the land,* and *wrath* is specifically *upon this people* (v. 23). But our verse of interest is verse 24, and particularly that last part:

...and Jerusalem shall be trodden down of the Gentiles, until the times of the Gentiles be fulfilled.   Luke 21:24

The Gentiles are the non-Jewish nations. We've been living in the times of the Gentiles since AD 70. Forty years after Jesus made His prediction, Jerusalem was destroyed by the Roman armies, just as He said. And for nearly two-thousand years, until the Six Day War of 1967, Jerusalem remained in the hands of non-Jewish, or Gentile powers. To this day, its population is divided between Jew and Gentile, with the city's status in a state of tug o' war between Israel and the United Nations.

Also known as the age of grace, due to the work of Christ on the cross, these are the times of the gospel to the nations. In his letter to the Romans, the apostle Paul also mentions these times of the Gentiles in relation to Israel's rejection of Jesus.

Romans 11:25 For I would not, brethren, that ye should be ignorant of this mystery, lest ye should be wise in your own conceits; that blindness in part is happened to Israel, until the fullness of the Gentiles be come in.

Once the fullness of the Gentiles arrives, Israel's blindness will be removed.

Zechariah 12:10 And I will pour upon the house of David, and upon the inhabitants of Jerusalem, the spirit of grace and of supplications: and they shall look upon me whom they have pierced, and they shall mourn for him, as one mourneth for his only son, and shall be in bitterness for him, as one that is in bitterness for his firstborn.

This transition from Jesus to Paul regarding the Gentiles provides a good introduction into some of the other details related to His coming. The apostle Paul has given us some additional identifiers to look for before the return of Jesus Christ.

2nd Thessalonians 2: The Apostasy

2nd Thessalonians 2:1 And, brothers, we entreat you, by the coming of our Lord Jesus Christ, and of our gathering together to Him, 2:2 for you not to be quickly shaken in the mind, nor to be disturbed, neither through a spirit, nor through speech, nor through letter, as through us, as if the Day of Christ has come. 2:3 Do not let anyone deceive you in any way, because that Day will not come unless first comes the falling away, and the man of sin is revealed, the son of perdition, ...(LITV)

At the time this was written, a falsehood had worked its way into the Thessalonian church making people think that the day of Christ had come.[xxxix] In addressing this issue, Paul reminded them not to be *deceived*. Verse 3 is our focus here. It says *that Day will not come unless first comes the falling away*. The Greek word for *falling away* is *apostasia,* meaning departure, or defection.[xl] In this context, it is departure from the truth (2:10-12), and is called "the apostasy" (or the "Great Apostasy," as some prefer). The Spirit, through the apostle Paul, also warned about this coming time in Paul's second letter to Timothy.

2nd Timothy 4:3 For the time will come when they will not endure sound doctrine; but after their own lusts shall they heap to themselves teachers, having itching ears; 4:4 And they shall turn away their ears from the truth, and shall be turned unto fables.

The Greek word translated *fables* also means stories or narratives (true or imaginative), fiction, or falsehoods, depending on the context.[xli] The idea here is that they will turn *from the truth* to listen to something other than the truth.

Although church history has seen times of departure from biblical truth through unbiblical teachings and traditions (1st Timothy 4:1-3),[xlii] the Bible itself had always remained the unquestioned authority and was revered as the Word of God. But this began to change during the age of the European Enlightenment of the 17th and 18th centuries. It was during this time that some people in influential positions began to question the truthfulness of Scripture, and formed their own ideas about God as they elevated the power of their own reasoning.[xliii] This shift in authority, from the Bible to human reasoning, marks the beginning of the departure that led into the apostasy.

By the 19th century, certain German "scholars," with such names as Johann Christoph Doederlein (1746-1792), Bernard Duhm (1847-1928), Julius Wellhausen (1844-1918), among others, began to dissect the Scriptures, viewing them as common pieces of uninspired literature. They denied the power of God and invented new ideas as to how the different books of the Old Testament came to be; none of which is factually substantiated (but was highly sensationalized). Doederlein, because he rejected predictive prophecy, decided that the book of Isaiah was written by two different authors: Isaiah, and some other fellow from Doederlein's imagination (known as Deutero-Isaiah). Later, Bernard Duhm fancied another unknown author and added him to Isaiah (Trito-Isaiah). Julius Wellhausen became famous for the "documentary hypothesis," in which he credited the writings of Moses to his four imaginary friends, "J, E, P, and D."[xliv]

These hypotheses are presented with a scholarly appeal. But strip away the sophisticated terminology, and it's the serpent all over again, questioning God's Word. But this time it isn't in a garden.

Others followed this trend into the twentieth century, creating a snowball effect; and this wave of disbelieving God that began with the Enlightenment spread throughout Western Europe and into Britain, finally reaching the United States and around the world.

Today these fabrications are found in liberal[xlv] and critical Bible commentaries, as well as the footnotes and introductory notes of liberal study Bibles,[xlvi] and are taught in seminaries, colleges and universities to those who preach in the churches and go out into the mission field. God became viewed as an evolving idea rather than a Person, and the *apostasy* was well under way.

This era also coincides with the rise of Charles Darwin's *Origin of Species* (1859) and his theory of evolution, at the height of British global power and influence. So powerful and pervasive was this lie that even conservative biblical theologians began to include forms of a "theistic evolution" into their works.[xlvii]

In 1917 Russia fell to atheistic communism. 1933 saw the publication of the first *Humanist Manifesto* in the United States. Its first and primary point denies creation, thus denying the Creator. Drawing from Darwin's theories, its second point states that man emerged as a natural process of nature.

Keep in mind that this shift in foundational beliefs took place among the so-called "Christian" nations. By the mid-twentieth century, evolution became a staple in children's education in the United States, while prayer and Bible reading were removed from their schools. Secular humanism replaced the collective biblical mindset, and the culture that once proclaimed Christ to the nations had turned away from God and His Word. The apostasy is here. The antichrist is next. It's *when we are*.

2nd Thessalonians 2: The Man of Sin

In Daniel 7, he is called the *little horn* who speaks great things against God (Dan. 7:8, 25), and makes war against the saints of God (7:21, 25). In Daniel 11 he is called the willful king, who does according to his own will:

Daniel 11:36 And the king shall do according to his will; and he shall exalt himself, and magnify himself above every god, and shall speak marvellous things against the God of gods, and shall prosper till the indignation be accomplished: for that that is determined shall be done.

Both passages describe the same person: the coming world ruler who will reign until the second coming of Jesus Christ. Here in 2nd Thessalonians 2 he is called the *man of sin*.

2nd Thessalonians 2:3 Let no man deceive you by any means: for that day shall not come, except there come a falling away first, and that man of sin be revealed, the son of perdition;

The apostasy (or *falling away*, as our King James has it) is the necessary precursor to the antichrist. This cultural shift away from the truth of the gospel and toward godlessness and sin serves to fill the earth with many antichrists (1st John 2:18-19), from which this *man of sin* will arise. At the same time it builds a godless world among humanity that will welcome, and even embrace this person once he arrives. In our time, it has become a norm for people to openly oppose Christianity and the God of the Bible. If this trend continues, the arrival of this *son of perdition* will likely be celebrated as a joyous occasion across the globe.

2nd Thessalonians 2:4 Who opposeth and exalteth himself above all that is called God, or that is worshipped; so that he as God sitteth in the temple of God, shewing himself that he is God.

This is the probably the most revealing description of the coming antichrist in the Word of God. It agrees with the descriptions found in the book of Daniel (chpts. 7, 11), but adds a missing ingredient: *that he as God sitteth in the temple of God, shewing himself that he is God.* This is very specific. Here we learn that this antichrist will sit *in the temple of God.* The Greek word translated, *sitteth,* can also mean having a fixed abode.[xlviii] He may actually *abide* in the temple.

Because the people of Israel had been separated from their land for nearly two thousand years, some Christians over the centuries have held that this reference to *the temple of God* means our bodies (as temples - 1st Cor. 3:16-17; 6:19). The idea was (and still is with some) that this *man of sin* (understood as our flesh, or sinful nature), would abide and be exalted in the hearts of people. He would be *revealed* in those who show, by their actions, their true nature (*by their fruits ye shall know them* – Matt. 7:20). And again, taken collectively as a body of individuals as a *temple* (2nd Cor. 6:16; Eph. 2:21), this phrase was also understood as meaning the church. The reference to Satan's seat in the church at Pergamos (Rev. 2:13) lends a measure of credibility to this perspective.[xlix] During the Reformation, many viewed the pope as the antichrist.[l]

But when we examine and connect the passages that describe this coming world leader (Dan 7:8, 20-21, 24-26; 11:36-45, 2nd Thess. 2:3-4, 8-10), there can be no mistake.

Today, Israel is a nation once again. The rebuilding of their temple is only a matter of *when*. And the time is also coming when that same temple will house *the son of perdition,* who will be worshiped as God. It is already written.

The Antichrist: Daniel 7, 11, and 2nd Thessalonians Comparison		
His designated identity	**His Activity**	**His End**
Daniel 7 **The Little Horn (7:8)**	Speaks great things (7:8,11, 20), wars against the saints and prevails (7:21, 25), opposes God (7:25)	Destroyed along with the 4th beast (global empire) at the coming of the Ancient of Days. Saints judge the earth. (Dan. 7:9-11, 21-22)
Daniel 11-12 **The Willful King (11:36)**	Exalts himself above God (11:36-37), no regard for God of his fathers (11:37), no desire for women (11:37), honors a god of fortresses (11:38), honors those who honor him (11:39), divides the land (11:39), brings war (11:40-45)	Prospers until the indignation is accomplished (11:36), will come to his end and no one will help him (11:45) at the time of the great tribulation (12:1), and resurrection (12:2)
2nd Thessalonians 2 **That man of sin, son of perdition (2:3)**	Opposes God, exalts himself above God, makes himself God by sitting in the temple of God (2:4), his arrival is the work of Satan (2:9), will produce signs and lying wonders (2:9), will deceive the unsaved world (2:10)	Destroyed at the coming of the Lord (2:8)

2nd Thessalonians 2: The Restrainer

2 Thessalonians 2:5 Do you not remember that I told you these things when I was still with you?
2:6 And now you know what holds back, for him to be revealed in his own time.
2:7 For the mystery of lawlessness is already working, only he is now holding back until it comes out of the midst. (MKJV)

We are now navigating into what has become a difficult passage. Once again, even the scholars of the ancient text have not adequately explained the meaning of verses 6 and 7, which deal with a *holding back* (also known as *the restrainer*). As we will see, the overarching difficulty in understanding these verses appears to be wrong focus, leading to wrong direction. And as we saw with Hippolytus and his misinterpretation of the four beasts of Daniel 7 (see chapter 2 of this work), this particular misfire likely began with another early church father named Tertullian (AD 125-220).

Tertullian was an early Latin Christian writer who believed this *holding back* (or *restraining*) was the Roman state. He further concluded that the *falling away* of verse 3 would be fulfilled by the dividing of the Roman Empire into ten kingdoms, which would thereby bring the *Antichrist* into this world. The following is a segment from his work, *On the Resurrection of the Flesh*, where we get Tertullian's understanding, which has influenced the viewpoint of the church throughout the centuries.

For that day shall not come, unless there first come a falling away," he means of this present empire, "and that man of sin be revealed," that is to say, Antichrist, "the son of perdition, who opposeth and exalteth himself above all that is called God or religion; so that he sitteth in the temple of God affirming that he is God. Remember ye not, that when I was with you, I used to tell you these things? And now ye know what detaineth, that he might be revealed in his time. For the mystery of iniquity doth already work; only he who now hinders must hinder, until he be taken out of the way." What obstacle is there but the Roman state, the falling away of which, by being scattered into ten kingdoms, shall introduce the Antichrist upon (its own ruins)? "And then shall be revealed that wicked one, whom the Lord shall consume with the spirit of His mouth ...."[li]

The Roman Empire has been gone a long time, and the *man of sin* has yet to be revealed. But while Tertullian was incorrect in his assessment, variations of his analysis have continued down through history. In his hindsight, Matthew Henry (1662-1714), understood the removal of the Roman state as opportunity for power and corruption to develop within the church so that by his time, the Pope was seen as *the man of sin*.[lii] But even those centuries are long past, and the end is not yet.

A relatively recent trend among leading evangelicals comes to us from *dispensational theology*, which was popularized by the *Scofield Reference Bible*. It holds that this *restrainer* is the Holy Spirit, who is actively *restraining* evil until He is *taken out of the way* at the rapture of the church.[liii] But this interpretation cannot be accurate either. Verses 1-3 tell us that *the coming of our Lord Jesus Christ*, and *our gathering together unto him* (the rapture) would not take place until after the *falling away*, and after *that man of sin* is revealed.[liv]

As already stated, wrong focus is the primary reason for not correctly understanding this passage. One reason for this is the way in which verse 7 has been understood and translated, and we will get to that when we arrive there. But in order to more correctly grasp Paul's intent in writing this section to the Thessalonians, we need to start at the beginning.

Back in verse 5, Paul reminded the Thessalonians that he told them *these things* before, while he was with them. *These* would be the *things* that he mentioned in the previous verses (1-4):

1. He began with the rapture - *the coming of our Lord Jesus Christ, and by our gathering together unto him* (v. 1).

2. He steadied the believers in regard to a present deception that was rising in their assembly - *That ye be not soon shaken in mind, or be troubled, neither by spirit, nor by word, nor by letter as from us, as that the day of Christ is at hand. Let no man deceive you by any means:* (vss. 2-3)

3. He reminded them of what to expect before the coming of Christ and the rapture - *except there come a falling away first, and that man of sin be revealed, the son of perdition;* (v. 3)

4. He provided specific details about *this man of sin*, also known to us as the antichrist: *Who opposeth and exalteth himself above all that is called God, or that is worshipped; so that he as God sitteth in the temple of God, shewing himself that he is God* (v. 4).

These are the things to look for before *the coming of our Lord Jesus Christ, and our gathering together unto Him*. Paul had told them these things while he was with them. And here he is reminding them again, in order that they recognize and avoid the *deception* presently at work in their midst. So in order to correctly understand Paul's message to the Thessalonian believers, we need to keep it local, recognizing that Paul's emphasis was directed against a then-present false teaching rising up in the midst of that assembly.

It also helps to understand that opposition and false teaching followed Paul wherever he went. While we don't have Paul's original spoken words while he was with these Thessalonians, we do have an example of what Paul told a different assembly of believers while being with them. His hearers in this instance were the elders of the church in Ephesus:

Acts 20:29 For I know this, that after my departing shall grievous wolves enter in among you, not sparing the flock.
20:30 Also of your own selves shall men arise, speaking perverse things, to draw away disciples after them.
20:31 Therefore watch, and remember, that by the space of three years I ceased not to warn every one night and day with tears.

And as it was in Paul's time, so it has been throughout history. The order is the same: truth first, followed by rebellion and falsehood. For there can be no rebellion against the truth where no truth is proclaimed. And falsehood prevails so long as it continues unexposed with no light to reveal it for what it is. But once the truth is proclaimed, the war begins; because Satan, who is the father of lies (John 8:44), is still the prince of this world (John 12:31, 14:30, 16:11; Ephesians 2:2).

Matthew 13:24 Another parable put he forth unto them, saying, The kingdom of heaven is likened unto a man which sowed good seed in his field: 13:25 But while men slept, his enemy came and sowed tares among the wheat, and went his way.

13:26 But when the blade was sprung up, and brought forth fruit, then appeared the tares also.

13:27 So the servants of the householder came and said unto him, Sir, didst not thou sow good seed in thy field? from whence then hath it tares?

13:28 He said unto them, An enemy hath done this.

Open rebellion against the truth in its various forms (silencing the messenger through violence, scandalizing the messenger's reputation, marginalization by intimidation, etc.), along with the workings of *counterfeit truth* (false gospels, false science or knowledge, etc.) begin to operate in order to undermine and supplant the truth. These are known conventional tactics of the enemy in spiritual warfare. These are things we can expect. And this is why Paul tells the Thessalonians not to be *shaken* or *troubled*. Satan's lies and strategies are self-evident to those who know and embrace the truth.

It is as though Paul reached down, picked up the snake from behind its head, showed it to them and asked, "Is *this* what has everyone so upset?" And having disarmed their apprehension by exposing the falsehood with the truth (which they already knew but needed to be reminded of - as we all do at times), he continues on the topic about which everyone is already familiar.

2nd Thess. 2:6 And now you know what holds back, for him to be revealed in his own time. (MKJV)

"And now you know" may also be rendered, *"and now you see."* The Greek allows for that. In fact, the Greek word translated, *know,* is *eidō* (εἴδω) and actually means, *to see, or to perceive with the eyes.*[lv] Once their eyes were open, they could *see* the "snake" for what it was, and no longer be *troubled* by it.

And now it is time for us to see the snake as well.

The original Greek word translated *holds back* here in verse 6 is *katechō* (κατέχω), and has several meanings. The following definition comes from Kittel's *Theological Dictionary of the New Testament*[lvi]:

Κατέχω

1. "to hold fast," "to hold back"
2. (spatially) "to occupy"
3. (juridically) "to occupy," "to hold in possession."

It is the same word used in Romans 1:18 for *holding* (KJV) or *suppressing* (MKJV and others) the truth.

Romans 1:18 For the wrath of God is revealed from Heaven against all ungodliness and unrighteousness of men, who suppress the truth in unrighteousness, … . (MKJV)

As *prince of this world*, Satan is not going to let go without a fight. He wants to *hold* on to what he considers his property. He *holds* people back from receiving the gospel and is continually at work *restraining* or *hindering* the gospel to keep people from fully grasping what it means.[lvii] So when we understand that *falsehood* was causing the *trouble* among the Thessalonian believers, we have identified what it is that was *holding back*, or *hindering* them; because Satan is the father of lies (John 8:44).

In his letter to the Galatians, Paul addressed this same problem, but in a different form, as those disciples were being led astray by adding the works of the Law to the finished work of Christ. Note the use of the word, *trouble*.

*Galatians 1:6 I marvel that ye are so soon removed from him that called you into the grace of Christ unto another gospel: 1:7 Which is not another; but there be some that **trouble** you, and would pervert the gospel of Christ.*

Paul told the Thessalonians not to be *troubled* (2:2). Paul wrote to the Galatians, who were being *troubled*. In both cases, the *troubling* influence was false teaching in the midst of their assemblies. Making *trouble*, *hindering* and *holding back* are all strategies of Satan to frustrate the gospel of Jesus Christ. Interestingly, Paul mentions that it was Satan who also held him and his companions back from visiting the Thessalonians on an earlier occasion:

1st Thessalonians 2:17 But we, brethren, being taken from you for a short time in presence, not in heart, endeavoured the more abundantly to see your face with great desire.
2:18 Wherefore we would have come unto you, even I Paul, once and again; but Satan hindered us.

False teaching obviously *hindered* Jude from writing what he originally intended to write:

Jude 1:3 Beloved, when I gave all diligence to write unto you of the common salvation, it was needful for me to write unto you, and exhort you that ye should earnestly contend for the faith which was once delivered unto the saints.

Jude 1:4 For there are certain men crept in unawares, who were before of old ordained to this condemnation, ungodly men, turning the grace of our God into lasciviousness, and denying the only Lord God, and our Lord Jesus Christ.

This *hinderer* is not some force of good *restraining* evil (the Holy Spirit, or God-ordained human government), but according to the context of both Scripture and the history of the gospel wherever it is preached, it is the work of Satan and his *hindering* through false teaching within the churches. It is a process which has been secretly working (*the mystery of iniquity, certain men crept in unawares*) from inside the church, by which the gospel is *restrained*, and the truth is *suppressed.*

As stated earlier (see *2nd Thessalonians 2: The Apostasy*), this process also prepares the world by producing many antichrists from which the *man of sin* will arise, thus creating a global culture where he will be quite at home, in his own element, and openly welcomed upon his arrival. Paul explained its working within the church. John shows the results going out from the church:

1st John 2:18 Little children, it is the last time: and as ye have heard that antichrist shall come, even now are there many antichrists; whereby we know that it is the last time.
2:19 They went out from us, but they were not of us; for if they had been of us, they would no doubt have continued with us: but they went out, that they might be made manifest that they were not all of us.

They went out from us, but they were not of us. And to this day, wherever the gospel is preached, and God's Spirit is drawing people to Jesus Christ, another spirit is continually working by deceptive means to not only steer people away from the truth of the gospel, but also to use them to spread the deception by which they themselves have been deceived.

And yet, what Satan uses for evil, God uses for our good. He allows for false teachings (or *heresies*) in order to test our faith.

Deuteronomy 13:1 If there arise among you a prophet, or a dreamer of dreams, and giveth thee a sign or a wonder, 13:2 And the sign or the wonder come to pass, whereof he spake unto thee, saying, Let us go after other gods, which thou hast not known, and let us serve them;
Deuteronomy 13:3 Thou shalt not hearken unto the words of that prophet, or that dreamer of dreams: for the LORD your God proveth you, to know whether ye love the LORD your God with all your heart and with all your soul.

As He did with Israel, so He does with us. God does not change.

1st Corinthians 11:19 For there must be also heresies among you, that they which are approved may be made manifest among you.

We now come to verse 7, which also requires some explanation due to possible mistranslation.

2nd Thessalonians 2:7 for the secret of lawlessness already works, only the [one] now restraining [will do so] until he may come out of [the] midst (LSV)[lviii]

We're working from the Literal Standard Version (LSV) here in verse 7 because it is close to the original Greek text, as can be seen from the Interlinear Greek New Testament below[lix]:

2Th 2:7							
το G3588 T-NSN ὁ the	γαρ G1063 CONJ γάρ assigning a reason	μυστηριον G3466 N-NSN μυστήριον a secret	ηδη G2235 ADV ἤδη even now	ενεργειται G1754 V-PMI-3S ἐνεργέω to be active	της G3588 T-GSF ὁ the	ανομιας G458 N-GSF ἀνομία illegality	μονον G3440 ADV μόνον merely
ο G3588 T-NSM ὁ the	κατεχων G2722 V-PAP-NSM κατέχω to hold down	αρτι G737 ADV ἄρτι just now	εως G2193 CONJ ἕως until	εκ G1537 PREP ἐκ from	μεσου G3319 A-GSN μέσος middle	γενηται G1096 V-2ADS-3S γίνομαι to cause to be	

The King James and most other English versions chose to translate the last clause of this verse to read, *until he be taken out of the way*. But the literal translation indicates an *emergence from the midst* of something, as circled in the illustration.[lx] When we read it for what it says, within the context in which it was written, this makes sense. It resonates with history as we understand it, and are currently experiencing in this confusing time of mixed messages: from different denominations and cults of Christianity, from world religions, and from a pseudoscience presented as fact on a global scale. The *man of sin* will emerge *from the midst* of a world filled with antichrists – the logical outcome of apostasy in its fullness.

104

This is sort of a polar opposite of what John the Baptist told his followers about Jesus:

Joh 1:26 John answered them, saying, I baptize in water, but One stands in your midst whom you do not know;
1:27 This One it is who has come after me, who has been before me, of whom I am not worthy that I should loose the thong of His sandal. (LITV)

As Jesus, who is the Christ (or Messiah), stood in the midst of a people seeking the heart of God, so the Antichrist will also rise from the midst of a people who are themselves anti-Christ.

In the following verses, the *hinderer* will be revealed as *Satan*[lxi], who is doing the work (of *holding back*, or *restraining*) by *suppressing* the truth and replacing it with deception, thus preparing the groundwork for his *man of sin* to step into the spotlight when his time arrives.

2nd Thessalonians 2:9 Even him, whose coming is after the working of Satan with all power and signs and lying wonders,
2:10 And with all deceivableness of unrighteousness in them that perish; because they received not the love of the truth, that they might be saved.

It is here that we are told that the *coming* of the antichrist *is after the working of Satan*. This *working* is accomplished through deception (*lying wonders*), and *with all deceivableness of unrighteousness in them that perish*: the false teachers (or the *tares*: Matthew 13:24-28). And this harmonizes with the warning at the beginning of the chapter (*Let no man deceive you by any means* – v. 3). Paul had told them this before, and here he is telling them again.

These Thessalonian believers ought to have known that this new and different teaching that popped up among them was nothing more than Satan at work to *hold* them *back* in their comprehension of the gospel and progression toward godliness. The entire passage is very well executed and would have been perfectly understood by its original recipients; as it also harmonizes perfectly with the teachings of Jesus (*wheat* and *tares* of Matthew 13; the false teachers of Matthew 24). And as we begin to understand this message as they did, at a point two thousand years after their time, we find ourselves at the other end, nearing its logical outcome.

And yet, this Satanic *restraining*, or *holding back* of the gospel message is only the result of the preaching of the gospel, which brings salvation to everyone who hears and believes it. Jesus had already told us that the end would not come until the gospel of the kingdom is *preached in all the world for a witness unto all nations* (Matthew 24:14).

That the man of sin has not yet been revealed may suggest that there are yet existing people groups to whom the gospel must be preached. The Internet and cell phones may expedite the process. But at the same time, the removal of prayer and Bible from children's learning, the removal of crosses and Bible references from public display, and a growing trend of labeling gospel preachers in terms of hate and intolerance in what were once Christian nations may be indicative that the *apostasy* is nearing its fullness, thus setting the stage for the appearance of this *man of sin*.

And we're watching it happen.

The Restrainer: A Scriptural Comparison

Scriptures are taken from the Literal Translation of the Holy Bible (LITV).

First the gospel is preached: first clause of Matt. 24:14	
Matt. 24:14	this gospel of the Kingdom shall be preached in all the earth
Followed by apostasy (falling away, false teaching, tares among the wheat): first clause of 2nd Thessalonians 2:3, 6 and 7	
2nd Thess. 2:3	first comes the falling away
2nd Thess. 2:6	the thing holding back
2nd Thess. 2:7	the mystery of lawlessness already is working, only he is holding back now
Resulting in revelation of the *man of sin*: second clause of each verse (and into verse 15 for Matthew 24)	
2nd Thess. 2:3	the man of sin is revealed, the son of perdition
2nd Thess. 2:6	for him to be revealed in his time
2nd Thess. 2:7	until it comes out of the midst.
Matt. 24:14 - 15	and then will come the end. (14) when you see the abomination of desolation (15)

2nd Thessalonians 2: The Strong Delusion

2nd Thessalonians 2:11 And for this cause God shall send them strong delusion, that they should believe a lie:
2:12 That they all might be damned who believed not the truth, but had pleasure in unrighteousness.

And for this cause: the reason that God sends *them strong delusion* is because *they* did not receive *the love of the truth, that they might be saved* (v. 10). Note the transition from *you* to *them* and *they*. Paul is not speaking of Christians here. By refusing God's free gift of everlasting life, and consequently having His Holy Spirit living in *them*, *they* chose the only other alternative. So instead of the Holy Spirit abiding in *them*, *they* get *all deceivableness of unrighteousness in them;* and *they* will *perish* (v. 10).

Choices have consequences. The greatest decision anyone can make who has heard the gospel of Christ is to believe it. And when we receive the truth of the gospel, we receive the Holy Spirit.

Ephesians 1:13 In whom ye also trusted, after that ye heard the word of truth, the gospel of your salvation: in whom also after that ye believed, ye were sealed with that holy Spirit of promise,
1:14 Which is the earnest of our inheritance until the redemption of the purchased possession, unto the praise of his glory.

Upon believing the *gospel* of our *salvation*, we are *sealed* with His *Holy Spirit*. Also called the Spirit of truth (John 14:16-17), He becomes our guide, so that we can avoid believing lies.

John 16:13 Howbeit when he, the Spirit of truth, is come, he will guide you into all truth

1st John 2:20 But you have been anointed by the Holy One, and you all have knowledge.
2:21 I write to you, not because you do not know the truth, but because you know it, and because no lie is of the truth. (ESV)

It is one of the ways of God to give people over to the full measure of what they choose. Choose Jesus and you get His Spirit living inside you, guidance into all truth, His promise of resurrection and life after death, His promise of a new and glorified body in His likeness. You become immortal. But your belief has to be real.

... for he that cometh to God must believe that he is, and that he is a rewarder of them that diligently seek him. (Hebrews 11:6)

And it doesn't matter when you mess up and sin along the way during your pilgrimage here in this life. Consider your sinful flesh as the same as a baby's diapers. They were made to get dirty. But they are not forever. And you are growing, having made the choice that supplies you with an Advocate with the Father, so that when we confess our sins, *He is faithful and just to forgive us of our sins, and to cleanse us of all unrighteousness* (1st John 1:9). We get the full measure of our choice when we choose Him.

And those who don't believe the truth receive the full measure of the alternative (Romans 1:21-32). Israel, for example, chose to worship other gods; so God gave them over to the full measure of idolatry and sent them to Babylon. And those who refuse to believe the truth of the gospel, God will give over to the full measure of believing lies.

In our time, much of Western culture has exchanged the truth of the Bible for the teaching of evolution and secular humanism. These are the mainstream lies in which many have come to trust and work to impose on the rest of our society. These lies have become foundational for these people's understanding of nature, biology, history, science, medicine, psychology, sociology, law and government, religion, and nearly everything else. [lxii] Open up just about any textbook, from elementary school to college, and this is what is taught. This is what *strong delusion* looks like in its fullness nearing the very end. It's *when we are.*

While this passage is certainly prophetic, we need to keep in mind that at the time it was written, it was an object lesson. Paul used a specific false teaching that had begun to circulate among the Thessalonian believers to help them recognize the working of Satan in the church, and how that working has for its purpose the unveiling of *the man of sin* when the time is right. That some among them would follow after the false teaching (*believing the lie*) would be indicative that they likely *received not the love of the truth that they might be saved.* This is what they were dealing with at that time. And in that sense, the working of Satan in the church has unveiled many *men of sin.*

What happened in Thessalonica was merely part of a continual process that has been at work throughout the ages, in order to prepare this world for the arrival of the antichrist. The mass deception that we are witnessing in our time-segment of this ongoing process as it nears its final destination is nothing more than the expected outcome of what began in Paul's time, roughly 2000 years ago.

Matthew 24 / 2nd Thessalonians 2 Comparison

While the table below compares the verses of Matthew 24 and 2nd Thessalonians 2 in order to demonstrate their similarities and order of events, it should also be remembered that some of these have been happening simultaneously over the centuries, have increased together and will continue up to the revelation of the *man of sin.*

Matthew 24 / 2nd Thessalonians 2 Comparison	
Matthew 24:10-15	**2nd Thessalonians 2**
24:10 And then many will fall away (ESV)	2:3 except there come a falling away first (apostasy)
24:11 False prophets, mass deception	2:11 strong delusion, people believe a lie
24:12 abounding iniquity	2:12 pleasure in unrighteousness
24:14 gospel of the kingdom preached in all the world	2:6-7 The man of sin kept from being revealed before his time
24:15 abomination of desolation in the temple	2:8 that Wicked revealed 2:4 in the temple of God declaring himself to be God

1st Thessalonians 4: The Rapture

1st Thessalonians 4:16 For the Lord himself shall descend from heaven with a shout, with the voice of the archangel, and with the trump of God: and the dead in Christ shall rise first:
4:17 Then we which are alive and remain shall be caught up together with them in the clouds, to meet the Lord in the air: and so shall we ever be with the Lord.

The word, "rapture," as it relates to the passage above (*caught up*), comes to us from the Latin root, *rapio,* which carries a meaning of "seizing," or "snatching up." We get our word, "raptor," (or bird of prey) from this Latin root. Likewise, the original Greek word from which our text above is translated, is *harpazo,* and also means to "snatch up" or to "seize." And it is from this word that we get another word for a bird of prey, "harpy." Both are the same, and a time is coming when believers who are alive at Christ's return will be "snatched up," or "raptured" into the clouds *to meet the Lord in the air* (4:17).

This is the rapture, and the Bible teaches it. While there is no question that the rapture is an event that will happen, biblical scholars do dispute the timing as to when it will occur. Our purpose here is merely to find out when the rapture occurs biblically. As we will see, the rapture is a shared part of the *parousia,*^{lxiii} that great appearing of our Lord Jesus Christ in the clouds of heaven. And as we have already seen, that day will not come until after the *apostasy* (the *falling away* from the faith), and after or about the time that the *man of sin* is revealed (2nd Thess. 2:3).

His Coming: Order of Events

1ˢᵗ Thessalonians 4:15 For this we say unto you by the word of the Lord, that we that are alive, that are left unto the coming of the Lord, shall in no wise precede them that are fallen asleep. 4:16 For the Lord himself shall descend from heaven, with a shout, with the voice of the archangel, and with the trump of God: and the dead in Christ shall rise first: (RV)

The topic of this passage is *the coming of the Lord*, with the order of events at His coming. The greater phrase, *we that are alive, that are left unto the coming of the Lord* means just what it says: we who are alive and remain until Christ returns. There will be no rapture before He returns. And then it says, *shall in no wise precede them that are fallen asleep*. The rapture of living Christians will not come before those Christians who have died. This means that their resurrection will come first, as emphasized at the end of verse 16: *the dead in Christ shall rise first.* And this will be a noisy event. The Lord descending from heaven with a shout and a trumpet blast is not the same as the sudden and mysterious disappearance that so many believe in our times.

1ˢᵗ Thessalonians 4:17 then we that are alive, that are left, shall together with them be caught up in the clouds, to meet the Lord in the air: and so shall we ever be with the Lord. (RV)

This is the order: the Lord descends, the dead in Christ rise first, and then the rapture. And these are to be taken as words of comfort:

1ˢᵗ Thessalonians 4:18 Wherefore comfort one another with these words.

The Last Trumpet

1ˢᵗ Corinthians 15:51 Behold! I tell you a mystery. We shall not all sleep, but we shall all be changed,
15:52 in a moment, in the twinkling of an eye, at the last trumpet. For the trumpet will sound, and the dead will be raised imperishable, and we shall be changed. (ESV)

The word, rapture, does not appear in this text, but it's talking about the same thing we just read in 1ˢᵗ Thessalonians 4. The order is the same: *trumpet* first, then the *dead* are *raised imperishable*, and *we shall be changed.*

Unlike the passage in 1ˢᵗ Thessalonians 4, which covers the event of His coming, here in 1ˢᵗ Corinthians 15, the emphasis is on one part of that event: the resurrection (see vss. 12-54). The overall context (vss. 35-54) stresses the difference between our physical bodies that we have now in this life, and the spiritual bodies we will receive at the resurrection. While 1st Thessalonians says we will be *caught up,* here we are told that *we shall be changed.* Our mortal bodies will be transformed into immortal bodies as we are *caught up,* or raptured. And it says that it all happens in an instant; *at the last trumpet.*

There is only one *last trumpet* in the Bible. We find it in the book of Revelation.

Revelation 11:15 And the seventh angel sounded; and there were great voices in heaven, saying, The kingdoms of this world are become the kingdoms of our Lord, and of his Christ; and he shall reign for ever and ever.

If the last trumpet of 1st Corinthians 15:52 is the same as the seventh trumpet of Revelation, then that means the first six trumpets, along with their plagues, will have already taken place before the resurrection/rapture event. In Matthew 24, Jesus stated that His glorious appearing, with the gathering of His elect will take place after the tribulation:

Matthew 24:29 Immediately after the tribulation of those days shall the sun be darkened, and the moon shall not give her light, and the stars shall fall from heaven, and the powers of the heavens shall be shaken:
24:30 And then shall appear the sign of the Son of man in heaven: and then shall all the tribes of the earth mourn, and they shall see the Son of man coming in the clouds of heaven with power and great glory.
24:31 And he shall send his angels with a great sound of a trumpet, and they shall gather together his elect from the four winds, from one end of heaven to the other.

Jesus said that His appearing will be *immediately after the tribulation of those days*, when the *sun* is *darkened* and *the moon* does *not give her light*, and *the stars fall from heaven*. It says that *all of the tribes of the earth* shall *mourn*, and that *they shall see the Son of man coming in the clouds of heaven with power and glory.*

This is His glorious appearing, *the Parousia*, with the *sound of a trumpet*, and the *gathering together* of His elect: the same ingredients that are found in both 1st Corinthians 15:52 and 1st Thessalonians 4:16-17. And Jesus said it will happen *after the tribulation of those days.*

The Rapture: A Scriptural Comparison

Christ in the Clouds	Sound of a Trumpet	Dead in Christ Rise First	Living Saints Raptured
Matthew 24:30 Son of man coming in the clouds	Matthew 24:31 sound of a trumpet	Matthew 24:31 gathering of the elect	
Mark 13:26 Son of man coming in the clouds	Mark 13 No mention	Mark 13:27 gathering of the elect	
Luke 21:27 Son of man coming in a cloud	Luke 21 No mention	Luke 21 No mention	
1st Thess. 4:16-17 Lord descends from heaven, elect are caught up into the clouds to meet the Lord in the air	1st Thess.4:16 the trump of God	1st Thess. 4:16 Dead in Christ rise first	1st Thess. 4:17 We who are alive and remain caught up with them in the clouds
1st Cor. 15:52 No mention	1st Cor. 15:52 the last trump	1st Cor. 15:52 dead raised incorruptible	1st. Cor. 15:52 we shall be changed
Revelation 1:7 Behold, He cometh with the clouds	*Revelation 11:15-18 the seventh trumpet	*Revelation 14:14-16 Son of man on cloud reaps harvest of the earth	

*The Revelation passages mentioning the final trumpet accompanied with the time of the dead in relation to rewards (11:18 – prophets, saints, all who fear God's Name, both small and great), and Christ on the clouds (Son of man) reaping the harvest of the earth (14:14-16) are separated by a two chapter interlude that focuses on Satan and his two beasts, followed by the first 12 verses of chapter 14 dealing with the 144,000 and the three angels.

Those Accounted Worthy

At this point we should take care to recognize that we are still in uncharted waters. All of this is future, and has not been experienced. We have the Scriptures which provide a fair amount of instruction, but we don't know how it will all be played out.

So while it appears that the rapture will take place at His coming after the tribulation (or more technically, the tribulation *of those days* – Matt. 24:29), there are two verses in the New Testament indicating that some will escape the tribulation *before* His return. The first passage is found in the gospel of Luke, and the other is in Revelation. One instructs; the other is a promise. Both are the words of Jesus Christ.

Luke 21:36 Watch ye therefore, and pray always, that ye may be accounted worthy to escape all these things that shall come to pass, and to stand before the Son of man.

According to Jesus, there is the possibility to be *accounted worthy to escape all these things that shall come to pass.* He tells us to *watch* and *pray always that ye may be accounted worthy.* We should be doing these things anyway, by virtue of His Spirit residing within us, but it seems that many professing "Christians" are involved in other pursuits. So *watch and pray.* And if you don't know what that entails, you might want to start seeking the mind of God through His Holy Word. It may take a lifetime, but there are worse things than struggling to reach the heart of God.

The other passage, which is a promise of reward, is in the book of Revelation:

Revelation 3:10 Because you have kept my word about patient endurance, I will keep you from the hour of trial that is coming on the whole world, to try those who dwell on the earth. (ESV)

This *hour of trial* that is coming upon *the whole world* is very likely the great tribulation. And Jesus promises that He will *keep* these people who patiently endured *from* that *hour of trial*. He does not say through it. He says *from* it.

So we have these two passages that reveal the possibility of escaping the great tribulation. And both place the responsibility of escape, not on the position of the believer in Christ as a guarantee (as in the resurrection/rapture event), but squarely on the shoulders of the believer to *watch*, to *pray always*, and to *endure steadfastly*.

We are not told how these faithful ones will escape the tribulation, but the Old Testament offers at least two possibilities. Genesis chapter 5 tells the story of a man who did not die. His name was Enoch. Enoch was removed from the earth long before God's wrath was poured out (the Great Flood). Here's what the text says:

Genesis 5:24 And Enoch walked with God: and he was not; for God took him.

Unlike all of those who died in the book of Genesis, it looks like Enoch just disappeared. Remember that watching, praying, and enduring are the ways of escaping the evil time to come. And Enoch *walked with God*. Who are you walking with?

Another example of escaping the coming tribulation is through death. Our example comes from 2nd Kings 22:8-20. The book of the Law had been found in the temple, and it was read before the king of Judah. He discovered that since the people had not been faithful to God that they were under the wrath of God. The king was Josiah, and unlike most of the people of Judah, Josiah was faithful to God. Here is the message he received.

2nd Kings 22:19 Because thine heart was tender, and thou hast humbled thyself before the LORD, when thou heardest what I spake against this place, and against the inhabitants thereof, that they should become a desolation and a curse, and hast rent thy clothes, and wept before me; I also have heard thee, saith the LORD.
22:20 Behold therefore, I will gather thee unto thy fathers, and thou shalt be gathered into thy grave in peace; and thine eyes shall not see all the evil which I will bring upon this place.

Josiah was told that he would die before the LORD unleashed His wrath upon Judah, so that he would *not see all the evil which* [the LORD would] *bring upon this place* (22:20). And so Josiah died before God's wrath fell upon Judah. We need to be like Josiah. His *heart was tender*; and he *humbled* himself *before the LORD*.

Isaiah also says something about the LORD removing certain people through death, to save them from the evil time that was coming.

Isaiah 57:1 The righteous perisheth, and no man layeth it to heart: and merciful men are taken away, none considering that the righteous is taken away from the evil to come.

It may be through death that the faithful few are removed to escape the coming trouble. We have the biblical precedent. We also have generations of Christians who have died and will never go through the great tribulation. Whether by a mysterious disappearance, or through death, or some other way, all we have are the words of Jesus; that He will keep some (those *accounted worthy*) from the time of trouble that will come upon the whole world. And He says to *watch, pray,* and *endure* to the end.

Daniel 7, 9 and New Testament Comparison

Daniel 7: Four Beasts/Kingdoms	Dan. 9 and New Testament
Rome 150 BC-AD 476 Winged Lion of Daniel 7:4	62 Weeks fulfilled (Dan. 9:25) 4-7 BC: Christ is born (Anointed One). AD 27 (approximate) Christ Crucified (Messiah cut off -Dan. 9:26). Christianity begins.
Byzantine Empire (Rome Divided) 330-1453 Bear of Daniel 7:5 Falls to the Ottoman Empire in 1453	AD 70 Jerusalem destroyed, Jews scattered (Dan. 9:26) Times of the Gentiles (Luke 21:24; Romans 11:25). All that Jesus said in Matthew 24:5-14 finds fulfillment throughout these times until His coming: Many proclaim Christ but deceive many (Matt. 24:5), Wars,
Islamic Empire 632-1922 Leopard with 4 Heads of Daniel 7:6 Rashidun Caliphate (632-661) , Umayyad Caliphate (661-750), Abbasid Caliphate (750-1259), Ottoman Empire (1300-1922).	earthquakes, famines, pestilences (Matt. 24:6-7) , Persecution (Matt. 24:9), Scandalizing and betrayal (4:10), Abounding Iniquity (Matt. 24:10, 12), Many False prophets (24:11) , Many Antichrists (1st John 2:18-22; 4:3)
European Global Colonialism 1492-1999: Beast with 10 horns of Daniel 7:7 1922 Ottoman Empire Ends 1999 – Macau is the last European colony decolonized	European Colonization facilitates Gospel preached to all the world (Matt. 24:14) Apostasy/Liberal theology ("Falling Away" of 2nd Thess. 2:2-3, 2nd Tim. 4:3-4) 1700s-Present 1948 – Israel a nation again. 1967: Israel and Jerusalem together again: awaiting command to rebuild Jerusalem for the 7 Weeks (49 yrs.) countdown to *the prince that shall come. (*Dan. 9:25) Strong delusion (2nd Thess. 2:11-12) Our Time Now –Gospel still preached
Our Time Now Uncharted Territory:	Uncharted territory: Gospel of the kingdom preached to all nations Watchful and prayerful taken out before the tribulation (Luke 21:36, Rev. 3:10) 7 Weeks Prophecy (*the prince that shall come* -Dan.
Little Horn King: Speaks out against God, Wars with saints of God. (Dan. 7:24-25)	7:25-26) 49- year countdown to the *coming leader.* Final Week Seven year covenant. Abomination of Desolation & Man of sin revealed in the Temple. Final 3 ½ years (Dan 9:27, Math. 24:15; 2nd Thess. 2:3-4) Great Tribulation Last repentance (2nd Peter 3:9), Fullness of the Gentiles (Luke 21:24, Romans 11:25)
God's kingdom comes. Judgment given to the saints. (Daniel 7:21-22; 26-27)	Return of Christ, Resurrection/Rapture (Matt. 24:29-31; 1st Thess. 4:15-17) 70 Weeks of Daniel 9:27-30 Fulfilled

Some Additional Thoughts

Introduction

In this section I have added some comments and biblical analyses, which, although they lie outside the more historically defined perimeters of *When We Are* with its timelines, they are closely related. And these are to be regarded as such: thoughts and comments – with room for disagreement. Some of these are not my own, and maintain acceptance among many sound Bible teachers, and are also found in various theological works.

Included in this section is a comparison table demonstrating the prophetic analogy of the seven churches of Revelation which was popularized by the *Scofield Reference Bible*. Also included are two additional timelines (*1,000 Years as a Day Analogy*), which, though I believe are valid, are not expressly mentioned in Scripture as such. They are implied rather than directly taught, and it takes a measure of insight and biblical understanding to grasp their significance.

I have also added a section titled, *Thoughts on the Antichrist*, which explores some of the different ways Scripture addresses kings and kingdoms, the spiritual entities through whom they are influenced, and some ways a nation as an entity can make its own statements. The United States is used as an example.

Also included is a brief study of *The Two Beasts of Revelation 13*, and how they might compare with the references to the coming world leader found in other parts of the Bible, such as the *little horn* of Daniel 7, the *man of sin* of 2nd Thessalonians 2, and the coming *prince* of Daniel 9.

Finally, I have added a section on *Readiness*. As we are entering these final years as described in Scripture, armed with the understanding of *when* we are on God's timeline, it might be wise to make some kind of preparation in advance as these evil times are beginning to overshadow us.

Revelation 2 and 3: The Seven Churches

Seven Churches as Prophetic

God often uses real life illustrations for prophetic symbols. He did it with Abraham, Moses, and others throughout the Old Testament. So it should be no surprise when we find that Jesus does this as well. And He has chosen seven particular churches and placed them in a specific order according to their described conditions. Although these messages were directed to seven real churches at that time, they also apply to individual churches with similar conditions in any given time. And in hindsight, the overall church also shares similarities with these described conditions, in the same order, as it moved forward through the ages of what is now history.

The following table on the next few pages highlights some of these similarities. You will need a Bible to read the full texts of Revelation 2 and 3 as they are not included in this table.

While there are those who deny this predictive aspect of the seven churches, we should keep in mind that the entirety of the book of Revelation is prophecy:

Revelation 1:3 Blessed is he that readeth, and they that hear the words of this prophecy, and keep those things which are written therein: for the time is at hand.

The Seven Churches as Prophetic

Ephesus: Rev. 2:1-7	Historical Comparison
Positive: Labor, Patience, did not tolerate evil.	Apostolic church. Gospel spreads rapidly. New Testament being written. ***Evil not tolerated*** (see N.T. epistles, general instruction).
Tested *false apostles* and proved them liars.	False apostles addressed and tested (2nd Cor. 11:12-15; Gal., 2nd Thess. 2:1-3; 2nd Tim. 2:16-18; 1st John 4:1 and others).
Hated deeds of *Nicolaitans*. Greek word meaning: *Nico*- conquer; *laity*- the people	No militant church hierarchy, no ruling class – see Mark 10:43-44. 3rd John 9-11 provides an example
Negative: Left first love	Left first love: see Acts 6:1-6; 15:1-5; 1st Corinthians; James 2:1-4, etc. Contrast Jn. 13:35

Smyrna: Rev. 2:8-11	Historical Comparison
Positive (?): *Tribulation, poverty* (but they are rich). Blasphemy by those *who say they are Jews but are not.* They are *the synagogue of Satan*, who will also cast *some* of them *into prison*. They shall *have tribulation 10 days* (2:10) **Promise***: be faithful unto death, receive crown of life.*	**Persecution begins** with the Jews who rejected Christ (Acts 5:17-42; 6:8-8:3; 9:22-25; 12:1-5; 13:50; 14:19; etc.). Continues with the Romans. *Tribulation 10 days*: Christian history offers a reference to 10 waves of persecution under Roman rule from Nero to Diocletian.[lxiv]

Pergamos Rev. 2:12-17	Historical Comparison
Positive: Held fast to the name of Christ, had not denied His faith, martyrs of Jesus among them **(Antipas)** **Negative:** Satan made his throne among them (Satan's "seat": the Greek word is *thronos*, or throne). **Doctrine of Balaam** **Doctrine of the Nicolaitans**	Churches hold fast to the name of Christ, have not denied the faith, martyrdom continues. **Emperor Constantine** declares Christianity a recognized state religion, grants government buildings and pagan temples to the churches (building design still in use today). **Church compromised with state:** *Doctrine of Balaam* (Numbers 22-25; 31:16). *Satan's throne*: Constantine as *pontifex maximus*[lxv] presides over church councils. New age of church governance: *Doctrine of the Nicolaitans* – church hierarchy, separation of clergy/laity
Thyatira Rev. 2:18-29	**Historical Comparison**
Positive: Love, faith, patience, service. Last better than first. **Negative:** Tolerance of evil - **Jezebel**: sexual immorality, idolatry.	Churches flourish in **love, faith, good works** but **tolerant** of evil in the church. In 431, Council of Ephesus (home of the goddess Diana – Acts 19:24-35), recognized **Mary** as "Mother of God." The Lord's Supper evolves to become a literal "sacrifice." "Forbidding to marry" (1st Tim. 4:1-3): **imposed celibacy** on priesthood leads to logical outcome- **fornication,** illicit sexual activity (1st Cor. 7:8-9) **Icon veneration**: officially sanctioned in 843 by Empress Theodora (idolatry).

Sardis: Rev. 3:1-6	Historical Comparison
Negative: Has a name as though it is living, but it is dead. **Positive:** A *few* have not defiled their garments.	**Beautiful cathedrals.** Great outward appearance. But pride replaced humility in church leadership **The Great Schism** of 1054: Greek Orthodox and Roman Catholic Church split. Church persecutes Christians. Age of the crusades[lxvi] **Three popes.** 1409. Rivalry for power in the Church.

Philadelphia: Rev. 3:7-13	Historical Comparison
Positive: Has a little strength, Kept Christ's word, have not denied His name **Promise:** Will be kept from the time of trial that will come upon the whole earth.	**1450: Printing Press**: Bible printed. Biblical studies increase. **Protestant Reformation** 1500s **European Colonialism** 1492-1999 facilitates **Global Missionary Activity and Evangelism:** 1500s-2000s **Awakenings, Revivals, Hymn writing** **Christian Abolitionism: Slavery ends in Europe and European colonies**

Laodicea: Rev. 3:14-22	Historical Comparison
Condition: Claims to be rich, increased with goods, needing nothing - but is wretched, miserable, poor, blind, and naked **Counsel: buy** of Me [Christ] gold **tried in the fire**, that thou mayest be rich; **and white raiment**, ...that the shame of thy nakedness do not appear; and **anoint thine eyes** with eyesalve, that thou mayest see. Jesus will **chasten**. **Jesus** outside: **stands at the door.**	**Enlightenment** 1700s. Human reason elevated above Scripture leads to **Liberal theology** 19th - 20th centuries, Bible seen as completely human work. **Prosperity gospel,** 20th-21st centuries **Positivity** focused **Pride:** sin openly accepted in many churches and denominations **Self-centered**- entertainment and celebrity-preacher focused. Megachurches.

1,000 Years as One Day Analogies

2nd Peter 3:8 But, beloved, be not ignorant of this one thing, that one day is with the Lord as a thousand years, and a thousand years as one day.

Because this verse is part of a greater passage dealing with the timing of Christ's coming and the end of the world, it may be viewed in two ways. Obviously, it is a comparison between God's timing and our timing, and God is not bound by time as we are. But since this verse appears within the context of His coming, it may also be viewed as a clue, of which we are not to be *ignorant*.

The Seventh Day Analogy

The following are two passages from the earliest works of the Apostolic and Church Fathers which demonstrate how the early church viewed the statement above by Peter.

Attend, my children, to the meaning of this expression, "He finished in six days." This implieth that the Lord will finish all things in six thousand years, for a day is with Him a thousand years. And He Himself testifieth, saying, "Behold, to-day will be as a thousand years." Therefore, my children, in six days, that is, in six thousand years, all things will be finished. "And He rested on the seventh day." This meaneth: when His Son, coming [again], shall destroy the time of the wicked man, and judge the ungodly, and change the sun, and the moon, and the stars, then shall He truly rest on the seventh day.

Epistle of Barnabas Chapter XV (AD 100)

For in as many days as this world was made, in so many thousand years shall it be concluded. And for this reason the Scripture says: "Thus the heaven and the earth were finished, and all their adornment. And God brought to a conclusion upon the sixth day the works that He had made; and God rested upon the seventh day from all His works." This is an account of the things formerly created, as also it is a prophecy of what is to come. For the day of the Lord is as a thousand years; and in six days created things were completed: it is evident, therefore, that they will come to an end at the sixth thousand year.

Irenaeus, *Against Heresies* (AD 120-202)

Many people today scoff at the very idea of a six-thousand-year-old earth. The popular view is that the earth is billions of years old, based on the suggestions of secular scientists and their work with radiometric dating. In truth, scientists have never proven the age of the earth. The correct term is *acceptance*.[lxvii] It is "widely accepted" by scientists that the earth is roughly 4.6 billion years old. What they offer is a suggestion, with a consensus of scientists, based on known half-lives in radioactive decay. And this may be subject to change as often happens in this field of study; nothing solid here.

From known history, however, we have documented (written) human activity that reaches back to a neighborhood of around 3400 BC. The collective witness of that time has creation stories for what preceded their existence; including God, or gods, and the creation of heaven and earth, to include a global flood not long after that.[lxviii] There are, of course, varying local myths interwoven in the different narratives, but the basics are the same.

We can account for the varying local traditions in the same way we've seen them arise in more recent history, because history repeats itself. Within Christendom, as one example, we find various local stories and legends of saints which have been added over time, and are not in the Bible, including later traditions for Christmas and Easter that have nothing to do with Christ. While the basic elements of Christianity are shared by different people groups around the world, local traditions vary. So while local traditions also vary from the ancient Greeks to the Native Americans, the basic elements of shared truth are present: Creator, Creation and Flood.

The consensus of the most ancient civilizations from one end of the planet to the other all agree that the world was created not long before their arrival, and that they themselves descended from a first created man and a first created woman; created by a Supreme Being. We call Him God. These people did not make this up. They received the information from their predecessors, and either put it into writing, or kept it preserved through oral tradition.

From the Bible (as well as what can be gleaned from other historical documentation[lxix]), we can calculate the years from the time Jesus was born through the generations all the way to Abraham (Matthew 1:1-17), and all the way back to Adam (Luke 3:23-38). From Adam to Jesus we have about a 4000 year timespan. And we know that Jesus was born around 4 to 7 BC[lxx], making His birth a little over 2000 years ago.

This means that roughly six thousand years from Adam until now is behind us. We are at the dawn of the seventh thousand-year time period since Adam; or in God's timing, the seventh day, or the Sabbath.

The Third Day Analogy: Return of the King

John 19:19 And Pilate wrote a title, and put it on the cross. And the writing was, JESUS OF NAZARETH THE KING OF THE JEWS.

According to this analogy, as goes the King, so goes the kingdom. Jesus, as King of the Jews, was crucified, and He died. After that, His kingdom – His earthly kingdom of the Jewish people (His title on the cross), was destroyed. In AD 70 the Jews were scattered. And they stayed scattered until the year 1948, when Israel became a nation again. Nineteen years after that, Jerusalem once again became part of Israel.

Jesus was raised to life on the third day, before daylight. Likewise, His kingdom will also rise – on the third day. Two thousand years has passed, or as it is with the Lord, two days.

Hosea 6:2 After two days will he revive us: in the third day he will raise us up, and we shall live in his sight.

The third day is dawning. And the King is coming.

Mass Travel/Increased Knowledge

Daniel 12:4 But you, O Daniel, shut up the words and seal the book, to the end time. Many shall run to and fro, and knowledge shall be increased (LITV).

There are those who teach that this running *to and fro* and *increased knowledge* refers to people running around and increasing "prophetic" knowledge, or searching anxiously to understand the scriptures.[lxxi] This may be based on a textual variant from an ancient Greek translation of the Old Testament, known as the Septuagint (or LXX). It deviates from the Hebrew text and reads as follows (the deviancy is highlighted):

*Daniel 12:4 But thou, Daniel, close the words, and seal the book to the time of the end; **until many are taught**, and knowledge is increased. (LXX)*[lxxii]

To not omit the one translation in favor of the other, both translations are valid. It works either way; be it for those who prefer this *running to and fro* as seeking scriptural knowledge, or (as the context indicates), mass travel and increased knowledge as it relates to the *end time.* But to discount the latter in favor of the former appears equivalent, in my opinion, to one who has spent his entire life in a cave, unaware of the sweeping differences of today's world from every other age in human history. Throughout the history of the world, most people lived near their homes, farmed the land, and did not travel far. And although there were those who regularly traveled great distances (merchants, military, explorers), by comparison to most people in the world, they were few.

Knowledge was also limited. People knew their trades, how to farm the land, and they knew their religious beliefs. Some knew how to read and write, possibly more than our modern scholars will have us believe (ancient civilizations had public signs and notices, posted names of buildings, etc., providing evidence for a common reading populace). But there were very few technological advances by comparison to our times.

For close to six thousand years of recorded human history, most people did not travel far, and knowledge was very limited. Not so in our times. Many are running *to and fro*. Multitudes from all walks of life and from every part of the globe are travelling like never before. And they are travelling long distances; by jet (*knowledge shall be increased*). As they are travelling (through the sky), they might be using their cell phones, or playing some kind of video game, or watching a video on some other piece of technology; or maybe listening to music no one else can hear, without the presence of musicians, thanks to *increased knowledge* and the invention of ear buds, among so many other things.

Over the last fifty years, knowledge has increased exponentially. Advances in medicine, robotics, nanotechnology, outer space and deep sea exploration, laser communication, and so many other fronts it becomes mind boggling, marks our time now as different from anything this world has ever seen in all its history.

The angel said, *"Many shall run to and fro, and knowledge shall be increased."* He said that in connection to *the end time*. And here we are.

Thoughts on the Antichrist

Antichrist as a Nation

Luke 4:5 And the devil, taking him up into an high mountain, shewed unto him all the kingdoms of the world in a moment of time.
4:6 And the devil said unto him, All this power will I give thee, and the glory of them: for that is delivered unto me; and to whomsoever I will I give it.
4:7 If thou therefore wilt worship me, all shall be thine.

We have already examined some of the characteristics of the antichrist as a physical human who will appear in the temple as the *man of sin*. But we would do well to recognize that Scripture also speaks of *spiritual* kings and princes in positions of power over this world. In the passage above, Satan offered to Jesus *all the kingdoms of the world* if He would bow down and worship him. Jesus did not question the devil's assertion on this. He merely said, *"Get thee behind me, Satan: for it is written, Thou shalt worship the Lord thy God, and him only shalt thou serve"* (Luke 4:8).

With this in mind, we should consider that nations are controlled by spiritual entities. We have a Scriptural example for this here in Luke's gospel, but they are also found throughout the Bible. In the following example from Daniel 10, an angel was on his way to Daniel in answer to his prayer, but was *opposed* by a certain *prince of the kingdom of Persia*. It was after help arrived from *Michael* the archangel that this particular angel was finally able to get to Daniel. Here is what the angel told him:

Daniel 10:12 "Don't be afraid, Daniel," he said to me, "for from the first day that you purposed to understand and to humble yourself before your God, your prayers were heard. I have come because of your prayers. 10:13 But the prince of the kingdom of Persia opposed me for twenty-one days. Then Michael, one of the chief princes, came to help me after I had been left there with the kings of Persia. 10:14 Now I have come to help you understand what will happen to your people in the last days, for the vision refers to those days." (CSB)

From this account, we are given a glimpse behind the scenes, and the spiritual entities are exposed. These beings are the powers at work, influencing and manipulating the minds of people, thereby subjugating and using them to expand their realm of authority from the spiritual to the physical.

The apostle Paul also exposed them.

Ephesians 6:12 For we wrestle not against flesh and blood, but against principalities, against powers, against the rulers of the darkness of this world, against spiritual wickedness in high places.

The terms, *principalities* and *powers* are synonymous with nations. A *principality* is the realm of a *prince. Powers* is a term commonly applied to nations. The following phrase from a popular news source provides an example of this:

"Western powers seek unity against Iran...."[lxxiii]

In this statement by *Reuters News Agency*, the western powers are the western nations. Interestingly, the United States is commonly known as a "superpower."

So there are other things we should consider as we attempt to understand and interpret prophecy. Scripture also interchanges the terms, king and kingdom, to mean the same thing. Note the symbolism of the goat in Daniel chapter 8:

Daniel 8:21 And the rough goat is the king of Grecia: and the great horn that is between his eyes is the first king.

While this *rough goat* is said to be the *king of Grecia*, it has a *horn* which is revealed to be the *first king*. The Hebrew word for king (*melek*) is used in this passage for both the goat and its horn. The goat is a *king*, and its horn is its *first king*. Other kings would follow. There is a spiritual king, or kingdom (the *goat*), under whose authority are other kings (horns of the goat).

The nations that colonized the world, represented by the ten horns of the beast in Daniel 7:24 are called kings. But spanning over four hundred years, each of these nations (*horns*) had several human kings during this period. They were born, lived, died, and were replaced by their successors. Yet their kingdoms spanned the centuries. So there is more going on than what we perceive in the physical world, and we would do well to expand our field of vision. We know that the antichrist is coming, but presently the *spirit* of antichrist is already working.

1ˢᵗ John 2:18 Children, it is the last hour, and just as you have heard that antichrist is coming, even now many antichrists have arisen, by which we know that it is the last hour. (LEB)

1ˢᵗ John 4:3 And every spirit that confesseth not that Jesus Christ is come in the flesh is not of God: and this is that spirit of antichrist, whereof ye have heard that it should come; and even now already is it in the world.

If there were *many antichrists* when the Apostle John wrote that back in the first century, they have multiplied. Today they are everywhere. We find them on the news, in the schools, in our colleges and universities, in government, and even in the churches; they may be your friends, families and neighbors. And they used to be many of us who have since given our lives to Christ.

We are truly living in an age that is largely consumed by *that spirit of antichrist*. So as we look for a specific *person* to fulfill the prophecies of the coming *little horn* or *man of sin*, many of the character traits for which he will be recognized are already present in the spirit of our times. Recall the works of the *little horn* back in Daniel 7:25:

Daniel 7:25 And he shall speak great words against the most High, and shall wear out the saints of the most High, and think to change times and laws: and they shall be given into his hand... .

And he shall speak great words against the most High. As we have seen (*Second Thessalonians 2: The Apostasy*, p. 89), this trend began during the Enlightenment when human reason was elevated above the Word of God. By the early 1960s, the U. S. spoke *great words against the most High* through its Supreme Court when it removed the Bible and prayer from the schools of its children. The lie of evolution replaced the Bible as the source for human origin and found its way into nearly every branch of learning in America's compulsory educational system, leading to widespread atheism, agnosticism, spiritual emptiness, loss of purpose, and outright hostility toward a "God" in whom many no longer believe.

It says that he *shall wear out the saints of the most High*. The word translated, *wear out,* means *to afflict,* or to *harass constantly.*[lxxiv] We saw this characteristic in its infancy during our study of 2nd Thessalonians 2, where it is called the *mystery of iniquity,* suggesting a hidden or covert working of Satan within the church. Two-thousand years later, at our end of the spectrum, we've reached its logical outcome in the overt hostility toward Christianity in nations that once held to a biblical mindset. The stage is being set so that when the antichrist rises to power, he will openly persecute the people of God with the full approval of the people of this world.

Daniel 7:25 also tells us that he will *think to change times and laws; and they will be given into his hand.* This mention of *times and laws* must be very significant. It is not unusual for a new government to make changes in recognized special *times,* or local *laws* in its new or conquered territories. This has happened throughout history. What is not normal is taking the place of God Almighty and changing *His* times and *His* laws. And this is exactly what this monster is going to do. But in case you haven't noticed, it has already been ongoing, gradually and covertly, under the table; the way Satan operates.

This gradual *change* in the *times* occurred during the 19th and 20th centuries as the six-*day* time-span of creation was replaced with *years* numbering in the billions, of an *uncreated* universe; right under our noses. And so the *times* have been changed accordingly, and people believe it. Prophetic in Daniel's time, it has already happened and we've been living in it for about a hundred years.

Also notable is the change in the way we understand the *times* of recorded history. This change is recent, and has been ongoing over the past 30 years. The use of BC (Before Christ) and AD (*Anno Domini*, Latin for *In the Year of Our Lord*) is being replaced with BCE (Before the Common Era) and ACE (After the Common Era). At the time of this writing, both systems are in in use, but the trend is set: with the goal of erasing Jesus from history.

In changing times past, collective memory is being erased and replaced. Historic monuments are being removed, and names of roads and institutions have been changed, serving to erase the past more completely. Special times once set aside for recognition of things like Christmas, Easter, or honorable men of history have been transformed to recognize other things. The works of historic revisionists have made their way into the textbooks of colleges and universities, as well as the public school systems. Today's young people are learning a different history than that of their parents and grandparents. This is happening on a global scale.

As God is being removed from the popular mindset, His *laws* are also being *changed*. Throughout recorded history in every culture around the world, marriage meant one thing: the union of man and woman together as one flesh.

Genesis 2:22 And the rib, which the LORD God had taken from man, made he a woman, and brought her unto the man. 2:23 And Adam said, This is now bone of my bones, and flesh of my flesh: she shall be called Woman, because she was taken out of Man. 2:24 Therefore shall a man leave his father and his mother, and shall cleave unto his wife: and they shall be one flesh.

That was Genesis. That was God. Jesus, who is also God, confirmed this *law* that was established by God in the beginning, at the dawn of man.

Matthew 19:4 And he answered and said unto them, Have ye not read, that he which made them at the beginning made them male and female, 19:5 And said, For this cause shall a man leave father and mother, and shall cleave to his wife: and they twain shall be one flesh? 19:6 Wherefore they are no more twain, but one flesh. What therefore God hath joined together, let not man put asunder.

Ordained by God in the very beginning, this has now been changed by man through the spirit of antichrist at work in nations that were once considered "Christian." Of course, this is only one law, and Daniel specifies *laws* (plural). Another recent shift in *laws* comes to us in the form of redefining morality. This too finds its origins in 19th century thinking that sprung out of the Enlightenment. It is called Socialism, and it is dominant today. Socialism sees immorality in the different levels of income that people make. They call this "economic inequality." This is new. This is different. And this is wrong.

Qualities such as honesty, trustworthiness, faithfulness, and the like have always been standards of high moral character for both rich and poor; and really, they still are. The infiltration of these socialistic policies however, have subverted these and supplanted them with external qualities of monetary value; and have made use of skin color, nationality, race, and even sexual activity as a rationale for "redistribution of wealth." But this is nothing other than legalized robbery.

Another recent change in *laws* came with the internet and cell phones. The laws governing the world monetary system is experiencing a shift from the physical to the virtual, from cash transactions to internet transactions, with the gold standard being replaced by "cryptocurrency." This move toward a global monetary system requires personal identification in order to buy or sell. Interestingly, Revelation 13:17 already states that the time is coming when it will be mandatory to maintain some kind of "mark" (or identifying feature) to access the economy. We are nearly there.

Today's generation lives in a secular society. Godlessness is today's social order, resulting in the removal of laws that are now considered outdated. Western Europe and its former colonies (including the U.S.) have decriminalized the old sodomy laws; and as already mentioned, marriage has been redefined.[lxxv] Europe, with its colonizing nations, once acknowledged God. This new "spirit" of our times is definitely different. It is *diverse* (Dan. 9:24).

At the time of this writing, a popular American television program recently celebrated an 11-year-old boy on their show, hailing him as a trailblazing drag-queen kid.[lxxvi] More recently, a U.S. presidential candidate, while campaigning at a town hall meeting, endorsed procedures designed to transform human beings into the opposite sex to begin on children as young as eight years old.[lxxvii] And he was elected.

The character traits for which the *little horn* king or *the antichrist* will be known are already present and prevailing. We are only waiting for these common attributes to converge into a single person who will rise to power. This is *when we are* today.

The United States – a possible candidate

Daniel 7:8 I considered the horns, and, behold, there came up among them another little horn, before whom there were three of the first horns plucked up by the roots: and, behold, in this horn were eyes like the eyes of man, and a mouth speaking great things.

This may only be food for thought, but interesting enough for consideration. It states that this *little horn* rises from *among* the other horns of the same beast. During the European colonization, North America was colonized by *three* European states: Spain, France and England. All three were "uprooted" by their own European inhabitants that would become the United States.

England was uprooted by its own colonies in the American Revolution. France was uprooted when U.S. President Thomas Jefferson obtained the *Louisiana Purchase*. Spain lost Florida in the *Florida Purchase Treaty*, and later lost more territory to the U.S. through the Spanish-American War. Three horns were plucked up, and a new nation began to rise from among the horns, and it became powerful. It may be that the United States fulfills the prophecy of the *little horn,* but this is by no means a conclusion. There may be other possible candidates that might better fulfill the characteristics given in Daniel 7.

...and a mouth speaking great things.   -Daniel 7:8

The United States is also set apart from the rest of the world by the great statements it has made, such as this one, from its Declaration of Independence:

We hold these truths to be self-evident, that all men are created equal, that they are endowed by their Creator with certain unalienable Rights, that among these are Life, Liberty and the pursuit of Happiness.

In a world of kings and lords, popes and cardinals, peasants and slaves, this idea of all men created equal was different. It was new, and it was powerful. In Daniel's time, words like these would have been unheard of. But even today, any thinking person understands that all men are definitely *not* created equal.

Exodus 4:11 And the LORD said unto him, Who hath made man's mouth? or who maketh a man dumb, or deaf, or seeing, or blind? is it not I the LORD?

Romans 9:21 Hath not the potter power over the clay, of the same lump to make one vessel unto honour, and another unto dishonour?

The idea *that all men are created equal* is an unbiblical idea at best. In fact, the entire statement, with its so-called *unalienable Rights*, might be considered blasphemous; as if God had granted us certain entitlements. But statements like this may have been among some of the *great things* Daniel heard coming from the mouth of that *little horn.*

But these are merely some thoughts.

Popping up from among the other horns of European colonization, the United States was bold at its inception. Within fifty years it was telling those other horns through its Monroe Doctrine not to mess with the Americas, or face retaliation.

Great things; bold things; new and different ideas have defined the United States as different from all the other horns of the fourth beast of Daniel 7. But again, this is merely a consideration.

Daniel 7:24 ...and he shall be diverse from the first,

Certainly the United States qualifies as different. Its government, with its Constitution and Bill of Rights, was created to be different. Like the *little horn* rising, the U. S. rose from the ground up, and was set up as a concord agreement of representatives from the thirteen nation-states that were once colonies of England. As such, the states retained all rights and sovereignty as individual nations (free and independent states), and were to be free of a controlling federal government, with minor exceptions in shared common law (such as common currency and necessary regulations for intercourse between free and independent states).

Unlike the European states and other nations around the globe, whose people were rooted by ancestry or by forced conquest and invasion, the United States has historically been made up of migrants from other nations by open invitation. This is different. And although in recent years (a little over a century) the U. S. began to merge and involve itself with the European powers, today it is seen as the most powerful nation on earth, continuing the status of being *different*. Again, this is merely a consideration, but it does maintain a fairly solid foundation in factual information. There may be another nation or some individual that might have superior qualifications; or maybe it remains to be seen at a later time.

and he shall subdue three kings. — Daniel 7:24

The Hebrew word for *subdue* also means *humble*. It may be that England, France and Spain were *humbled* by the rise of this new nation. But the U.S. has also been involved in the subjugation of several nations. During World War II, Germany, Italy and Japan were subdued after the United States played a leading role in that war, in alliance with France, England and Russia.

But again, this is by no means conclusive. Indeed, for a time, Nazi Germany and Adolph Hitler might have made excellent candidates for the *little horn* and the *antichrist*. Before that, many Protestants viewed Catholicism and the pope in much the same way.[lxxviii] And many still do.

The Antichrist as a Person

Daniel 11:37 Neither shall he regard the God of his fathers... nor regard any god: for he shall magnify himself above all.

One of the identifiers of the *little horn* is that he will speak great words against God (see also Daniel 7:25). The individual in this verse will have no regard *for the God of his fathers*. The Hebrew word translated, *God*, is *Elohim* and can mean either God, or gods (plural), depending on the context. But since this is the *little horn,* rising from among the colonizing European nations, we may conclude that the God of the Bible is meant here due to the fact that European colonialism coincided with the Protestant Reformation in Europe, as well as the missionary movement that spread the gospel to the ends of the earth.

Today most of Europe and its former colonies no longer revere the God of their fathers in any official capacity, having fallen away from Christendom. But the United States owns the peculiar status of being the birthplace of Secular Humanism,[lxxix] which removes all honor and responsibility from God and places it onto man.

The popular rule of our time is that we humans are the deciders of our own collective destiny, and not God. So when this antichrist arrives on the scene declaring himself superior to God, it will be no different from what many people today already believe about themselves. This is *when* we are today as nations, and collectively as a "global community." It seems that "In God We Trust" is fast becoming the motto of a bygone age.

Daniel 11:37 Neither shall he regard the God of his fathers, nor the desire of women, …

That the antichrist will have no *desire of women* should create no alarm. Already there are politicians and world leaders who openly espouse various forms of sexual activity outside the bounds of traditional marriage between man and woman. It would likely be seen as a wonderful thing to have such an individual elevated to a high position. The world calls it "diversity" (*and he shall be diverse* – Daniel 7:24), and it is celebrated today. But having no desire for women does not necessitate a homosexual antichrist. Eunuchs have no desire for sexual activity; and as the sex drive declines with age, an older man would equally qualify for the title of an antichrist not desiring women.

The Digital Antichrist

Today's world is dominated by what is known as "Big Tech." Another consideration (which might be a stretch) is that this "person" may not even be human at all. He may be some form of artificial intelligence (AI). In the next section, we will examine the two beasts of Revelation 13. The first beast appears to be the coming world ruler we've been reading about. He will receive a deadly wound, and then is seemingly restored to life (Rev. 13:3, 12). But his restoration to life may be an illusion.

A *second* beast (Rev. 13:11-18) then takes over. This beast will be associated with worship, but will also be very influential in politics. He will have power to give life to an "image" of this first beast (Rev. 13:15), and will cause everyone to worship the image of the beast. Revelation does not provide a location for the activity of this *second* beast, but one possibility may be that some kind of artificial intelligence is placed in the temple, in the image of that first beast, and will become the abomination of desolation. This *second* beast who allows for this might be a Jewish priest or some other religious leader who will also be a major political figure.

Recall in Daniel 9:27 that a seven year covenant would be established, and halfway through that seven years (*in the midst of the week*), the sacrifice and offering would stop. It is then that the *abomination of desolation* appears in the temple. Jesus said that when this happens, there will be a time of trouble, the likes of which the world has never seen, nor ever will again (Matthew 24:15).

Neither Daniel nor Jesus (as quoted in the gospel records) reveals what this *abomination* is, or how it (or he) arrives in the temple. But 2nd Thessalonians 2:4 tells us that there will be a man in the temple – *the man of sin*.

Following the biblical progression, we find this *willful king* of Daniel 11:36-45, who exalts himself above all gods, and speaks out against the God of gods (Dan. 11:36-38). He will be a man of war, and will overpower three nations: Egypt, Libya and Ethiopia (Dan. 11:38-43, compare Dan. 7:24). Interestingly, he will also control finances (Dan. 11:43). But then it says that this willful king *shall come to his end* (Dan. 11:45); and the next sentence, Daniel 12:1, places the great tribulation *at that time*.

Daniel 12:1 And at that time shall Michael stand up, the great prince which standeth for the children of thy people: and there shall be a time of trouble, such as never was since there was a nation even to that same time: and at that time thy people shall be delivered, every one that shall be found written in the book.

When the *willful king* comes *to his end* (Dan. 11:45), that is when *the time of trouble* begins. And the signal event for this *time of trouble*, or *great tribulation*, is the appearance of the *abomination of desolation* of in the temple of God (Matt. 24:15). So one possibility is that he will be killed (*come to his end*), and then some image or likeness of him might be placed in the temple. Or possibly, through some form of medical technology, he may actually be given new life.

Marks of the Antichrist

Called *the little horn* in Daniel 7	Daniel 7:8
Arrives after the first 10 horns (or kingdoms)	Daniel 7:24
Will be different from the other 10 kings/kingdoms	Daniel 7:24
Will be a powerful speaker	Daniel 7:8, 20
Will seek to change times and laws	Daniel 7:25
Will be outspoken against God	Daniel 7:25; Rev. 13:6
Will not regard the God of his fathers, nor desire women	Daniel 11:37
Will make war with God's people (the saints), and prevail	Daniel 7:21, 25; Rev. 13:7
Called the *man of sin, and the son of perdition*, and *that Wicked*	2nd Thess. 2:3, 8
Will bring war, and will conquer	Daniel 11:40-42
Subdues 3 Kings (or nations)	Daniel 7:24; 11:43
Will have power over wealth	Daniel 11:43
Will reward those who honor him, making them rulers, and will divide the land	Daniel 11:39
Will be troubled by news from the north and the east (Russia? China?)	Daniel 11:44
Will make a 7 year covenant	Daniel 9:27
Will be killed and appear to be resurrected	Daniel 11:45 (come to his end), Rev. 13:3, 12 (deadly wound healed)
Will appear in the temple of God: the *abomination of desolation*	Dan. 9:27, Matt. 24:15, 2 Thess. 2:3-4
Will magnify himself above God, and all gods, declare himself to be God	Daniel 11:36; 2nd Thess. 2:4
Destined for destruction	Daniel 7:11, 26; 11:45; 2nd Thess. 2:8 Rev. 19:20

The Two Beasts of Revelation 13

The Technology

Revelation 11:8 And their dead bodies shall lie in the street of the great city, which spiritually is called Sodom and Egypt, where also our Lord was crucified.
11:9 And they of the people and kindreds and tongues and nations shall see their dead bodies three days and an half, and shall not suffer their dead bodies to be put in graves.
11:10 And they that dwell upon the earth shall rejoice over them, and make merry, and shall send gifts one to another; because these two prophets tormented them that dwelt on the earth.

The passage above from the first century stood for two thousand years telling the world that a time was coming when people of different tribes, nations and languages *shall see* the same event as it takes place in one city.[lxxx] At no other time in history could the entire world, all at the same time, view an incident as it was happening in one location as we can today. Certainly through television, part of the world could have done this in previous decades. But with the advent of cell phones, this kind of access has reached even the most isolated tribes. This is *when we are*.

As we peruse through the *Two Beasts of Revelation*, we will see a few things that should not surprise us in the least, other than the fact that they were foretold two thousand years ago. We live in the twenty-first century and understand something of missile and drone technology and the functional capacities of our cell phones. The Apostle John could only describe such things in first century terms. The book of Revelation is high-tech.

We are still in uncharted waters here, and so we cannot be dogmatic about too many of the details. We can, however, pay close attention to the Word of God as our compass to help us in our navigation.

The First Beast

Revelation 13:1 And I stood upon the sand of the sea, and saw a beast rise up out of the sea, having seven heads and ten horns, and upon his horns ten crowns, and upon his heads the name of blasphemy.
13:2 And the beast which I saw was like unto a leopard, and his feet were as the feet of a bear, and his mouth as the mouth of a lion: and the dragon gave him his power, and his seat, and great authority.

This is the first of the two beasts. The other one will appear down in verse 11. This beast has *seven heads*, *ten horns* and *crowns* on its horns, with *the name of blasphemy* written *upon his heads*. It is described as having the physical likeness of three predatory animals combined into one; the same three beasts we saw in Daniel 7. It appears that the beasts of Daniel 7 have combined together here in Revelation 13. If this is the case, then its *seven heads* may possibly be of the same combination: one head for Rome, one for the Byzantine Empire, one each for the four heads of the leopard (the four Islamic ruling dynasties), and one for the European empire (globalism). The total is seven. The ten horns with crowns (kings) might reflect the ten European nations that colonized the world, thus combining all four beasts into one. But this is only one way looking at this picture.

The *name of blasphemy* is written on its heads. We can only speculate as to what this *name of blasphemy* is. But every head (or kingdom) of this composite beast carries it, and every one of them is guilty as charged.

Observing this beast as a mixture into a single entity of all the beasts of Daniel 7, we might see a resemblance in our world today in the mixture of globalism. European people had entered into the nations of the world through colonization. Today the world is experiencing an unprecedented mixing of populations as refugees and migrants from those nations, with their diverse cultures and religious beliefs, are pouring into the European nations and their former colonies (United States, Canada, Australia, etc.). Multiculturalism and diversity are catch-words for our times. It appears that this *beast* is already present in today's world of multinationalism.

Revelation 13:3 And I saw one of his heads as it were wounded to death; and his deadly wound was healed: and all the world wondered after the beast. 13:4 And they worshipped the dragon which gave power unto the beast: and they worshipped the beast, saying, Who is like unto the beast? who is able to make war with him?

If this *beast* is a composite of all four beasts of Daniel 7, we are not given any distinction as to which of its *heads* receives the *deadly wound*. However, following the progression of what we have already studied, this *wounded* head may be that final stage of Daniel 7's fourth beast (European Empire), with the *willful king* in charge of it, who will also come *to his end* as stated in Daniel 11:45. It may be that he will be assassinated, and then possibly brought back to life (*his deadly wound was healed*).

This is not, however, to set aside the possibility of a restoration of the Byzantine or Ottoman Empire, or any of the other *"heads"* of this leopard-like beast that have ceased to exist (including the original Roman Empire). Whatever the case, it will be such an event that will cause *all the world* to *wonder,* or admire (as the Greek implies) *the beast.*

The really sad news is the focus of worship here. The world outside of Christ will worship Satan (*the dragon* – see Rev. 12:9). They will also worship *the beast.* And it appears that they do this willfully, without any external compulsion. Full allegiance to a nation can be very close to idol worship, and we have seen this before in Nazi Germany. Nor is this idea absent in the nation-centered anthems and love of country, which may easily become a form of idolatry. And national loyalty often leads to betrayal of friends and family, leading to lack of trust in fellow-citizens, close friends and relatives (Matt. 24:10; 10:36). So this is not too difficult to grasp. Neither is emperor-worship out of our reach in understanding. Today we see multitudes following certain individuals (celebrities, politicians), practically worshiping them as gods. It should never surprise us when history repeats itself.

The idea of global Satan worship, however, is more difficult to swallow. How that will come about (and it will) may possibly result through an integration of shared viewpoints of secular humanism, Buddhism, and those of various religions (including liberal Christendom) merging together. Today, Satanism is advertised using the same tenets of secular humanism, such as sexual freedom, reproductive rights, and enjoying this life to its fullest.[lxxxi]

Interestingly, a popular handbook for political activists, Saul Alinsky's <u>Rules for Radicals</u>, opens with an acknowledgement of what it calls, *the very first radical;* the devil himself:

"Lest we forget at least an over-the-shoulder acknowledgment to the very first radical: from all our legends, mythology, and history (and who is to know where mythology leaves off and history begins — or which is which), the first radical known to man who rebelled against the establishment and did it so effectively that he at least won his own kingdom — Lucifer."[lxxxii]

So there is, in political activism, a seed planted for a positive recognition of Satan. And Satan worship is now available, in an official, recognized capacity, in some of the leading nations today.[lxxxiii] Satan clubs in public schools are present in the United States. Universal Satan worship will happen. We're only waiting as the components come together that will make it happen.[lxxxiv]

The question regarding the ability to *make war with* the beast (13:4) seems indicative of the nation that the beast represents. Today it is the United States that boasts that level of power in warfare, and is recognized for this around the world. But the combining of all western nations into one entity would most certainly appear formidable. But this too remains to be seen.

Revelation 13:5 And there was given unto him a mouth speaking great things and blasphemies; and power was given unto him to continue forty and two months. 13:6 And he opened his mouth in blasphemy against God, to blaspheme his name, and his tabernacle, and them that dwell in heaven. 13:7 And it was given unto him to make war with the saints, and to overcome them: and power was given him over all kindreds, and tongues, and nations.

This passage is very much like the description of the *little horn* in Daniel 7, who has a *mouth speaking great things* (Dan. 7:8), and will *speak great words against the most High* (Dan. 7:25). And like this beast here in Revelation 13, who has power to *make war with the saints, and to overcome them*, the little horn in Daniel's vision also *made war with the saints, and prevailed against them* (Dan. 7:21). It is evident that this beast is the same individual as the *little horn* of Daniel 7, and also the *willful king* of Daniel 11 who also speaks out against God (Dan. 11:36), as does the *man of sin* of 2nd Thessalonians 2:4.

That he shall *continue forty and two months* (three and a half years) also corresponds to the *little horn* in Daniel 7:25's *time and times and the dividing of time*. This also agrees with the *prince that shall come* of Daniel 9, who makes a covenant for *one week* (seven years: Dan. 9:27); but in the *midst of* that *week* (three and a half years) the sacrifice and offering suddenly stops. The three and one-half year mark is likely the point in which this individual *comes to his end* (Dan. 11:45), when he receives this *deadly wound*. It is then that the *abomination of desolation* appears in the temple (Dan. 9:27), bringing us into that second half of the week (another three and a half years), which leads to the end.

And this is where it gets interesting; because nowhere else in the Bible up to this point (unless it is there but hidden), are we told of a *second* antichrist – a religious leader. He's coming up next here in Revelation 13. He is also known as the *false prophet* (Rev. 19:20). And his appearance comes after a reference to someone being *killed with the sword* (13:10).

Revelation 13:8 And all that dwell upon the earth shall worship him, whose names are not written in the book of life of the Lamb slain from the foundation of the world.
13:9 If any man have an ear, let him hear.
13:10 He that leadeth into captivity shall go into captivity: he that killeth with the sword must be killed with the sword. Here is the patience and the faith of the saints.

The Second Beast

Revelation 13:11 And I beheld another beast coming up out of the earth; and he had two horns like a lamb, and he spake as a dragon. 13:12 And he exerciseth all the power of the first beast before him, and causeth the earth and them which dwell therein to worship the first beast, whose deadly wound was healed.

Unlike the first beast, or the beasts of Daniel 7, which all rise up from the sea, this second beast comes up from the *earth.* The Greek word used for *earth* can also mean land, or even a country, territory or region. It may be a reference to the land of Israel, but we cannot be conclusive. It may be referring to the whole world, or *earth*, as our English has it. One word can change the entire meaning of a text. And we need to be mindful that we are sailing in uncharted waters.

The fact that this second beast has *two horns like a lamb* may indicate two nations, or two leaders. We are given no further physical description. We are told that it *spake as a dragon* and *exerciseth all the power of the first beast before him.* He is a political leader, and also a *worship* leader.

He *causeth the earth* [or *land*] *and them which dwell therein to worship the first beast, whose deadly wound was healed.* Here we are expressly told that the first beast will indeed be killed, or at least receive a *deadly wound* that should have killed it, and this dragon-voiced beast with the lamb horns will require *the earth* (or the land), *and them which dwell therein* to *worship* it.

If the land of Israel is what is meant here, this resurrected *first beast* may be the *abomination of desolation* that will be in the temple of God (Matt. 24:15; 2nd Thess. 2:4). But from this point on, it is the second beast that is in control.

Revelation 13:13 And he doeth great wonders, so that he maketh fire come down from heaven on the earth in the sight of men,

Again, when we read the events of Revelation, we understand that the descriptions come to us from the first century mind. John is describing things he knows nothing about in the best way that he is able. He has never experienced missile technology, lasers or satellites. But this verse should not surprise us in the least. What was a great wonder to the apostle John in the first century is everyday life for us today.

Revelation 13:14 And deceiveth them that dwell on the earth by the means of those miracles which he had power to do in the sight of the beast; saying to them that dwell on the earth, that they should make an image to the beast, which had the wound by a sword, and did live.

The world will be deceived by the *miracles* that this person will be able to do. And he will do these miracles *in the sight of the beast;* apparently referring to the first beast, that *head* of the leopard-like conglomeration which was *wounded to death* and then *healed*. The main thrust is in the mass deception, and how that is used to obtain the obedience of the people; as we so often see whenever we turn on the news. But at that time, everyone will *make an image to the beast.* And they will worship it.

Revelation 13:15 And he had power to give life unto the image of the beast, that the image of the beast should both speak, and cause that as many as would not worship the image of the beast should be killed.

These verses would have been a mystery in ages past. How could an *image* be given *life*, and *speak*? But the *power to give life unto the image of the beast*, like the *fire* falling *from heaven* (v. 13), is not such a wonder at a time when motion pictures have given *life* to many people who have died. And more recently, through CGI (computer generated imagery), the dead have been "raised" to both live and speak posthumously in motion pictures.[lxxxv] Incidentally, the Greek word translated, *image*, is *eikōn*. And people are already using icons today through our interconnected world on social media.

It may be through the use of cell phones that people will be required to make this "icon" *to the beast.* Computer animation with interaction through data or Wi-Fi and rapid automated response signaling might easily and quickly detect noncompliant individuals for elimination. For sailing into uncharted waters, things are beginning to look way too familiar as I write these words. But this is, after all, *when we are.*

The Mark of the Beast

Revelation 13:16 And he causeth all, both small and great, rich and poor, free and bond, to receive a mark in their right hand, or in their foreheads:
13:17 And that no man might buy or sell, save he that had the mark, or the name of the beast, or the number of his name.

For those who are not eliminated, there will be a requirement for identification in order to participate in the economy (*buy and sell*). It will come in the form of a *mark in their right hand, or in their foreheads.* The word, *mark*, in the original Greek is *charagma,* and means stamp, imprinted mark, or even a carved or sculpted work. A tiny, grain-sized object that may be implanted beneath the skin might qualify. Smart tattoos, now in development, are also a possibility. Or it may be referring back to that aforementioned *icon* in verses 14 and 15.

Note that the *mark* is not the only way to participate in the economy. If for some reason one does not have the *mark*, he or she may use *the name of the beast, or the number of his name* instead.

The fact that we use ID numbers for financial transactions is troubling. We have social security numbers, credit and debit card numbers, cell phone numbers, and others. In all the history of the world, people were never identified with numbers as we are today. So today, you can use your cell phone, or that chip on your card, or type in your number to make a transaction. In many places of business, it is the only way. We are well on our way to the time of the coming *mark* when it will be mandatory everywhere.

Speaking of how things become mandatory, there was once a time when having health insurance was considered a luxury. It later expanded to become a benefit employers offered to attract eligible candidates for employment. This practice increased, and it later became an expectation that employers offer health insurance to their employees. Finally, under Barack Obama's *Affordable Health Care Act*, having health insurance became mandatory in order to live and breathe in the United States.

The Covid-19 pandemic, with its global vaccine mandates and requirements for proofs of vaccination might be a wake-up call. This *mark* is coming, and it will be required. If for some reason, you find yourself still here during this phase of the end of the world, you do NOT want to get this *mark*. Here's why:

Revelation 14:9 And the third angel followed them, saying with a loud voice, If any man worship the beast and his image, and receive his mark in his forehead, or in his hand, 14:10 The same shall drink of the wine of the wrath of God, which is poured out without mixture into the cup of his indignation; and he shall be tormented with fire and brimstone in the presence of the holy angels, and in the presence of the Lamb: 14:11 And the smoke of their torment ascendeth up for ever and ever: and they have no rest day nor night, who worship the beast and his image, and whosoever receiveth the mark of his name.

Today, people are receiving chip implants. Although these are not the *mark* of the beast, they are certainly precursors to what's coming. Hopefully we will not be around when that time comes. But if you happen to be here, do NOT take that mark. Do NOT make that icon, or worship the beast.

But understand this: by not participating in the mandatory requirements imposed by Satan onto this world, you will likely suffer. You will not be able to buy food or receive medical treatment. Or you may simply be put to death, as the Scripture says. But you will be suffering on behalf of Jesus Christ, and He will reward you for it. And you will have your place in the procession of the martyrs throughout history, who also suffered for our Lord, who will have a place at His table when He returns.

And let's not forget that the persecutors throughout history have all died as well. Where do you suppose they are spending eternity? Food and medical care are only temporal until life ends, as life always does. We do not look to this life, which is temporal. We look for the next one, which is eternal.

Revelation 13:18 Here is wisdom. Let him that hath understanding count the number of the beast: for it is the number of a man; and his number is Six hundred threescore and six.

Throughout the centuries, men and women of all walks of life have endeavored to solve this puzzle of *the number of the beast*. That it can be solved is evident, but it is reserved for *him that hath understanding.* So far, no one seems to have unlocked the secret.

Conclusion

Although the things written here in Revelation 13 may not happen in the way I have explained, we can rest assured that they will come to pass, as Bible prophecy always does. With that in mind, it would be wise to take note of our own times and technology in relation to these things as described by the apostle John. What was prophetic in his time is quickly becoming all too real in ours.

Readiness: Our Posture in Light of These Things

The Welcoming Committee

The fulfillment of the *sixty-two weeks* portion of the Daniel 9 prophecy became history with the birth of Jesus Christ. But what makes this all the more interesting is that it may also provide insight into how some people knew that the time was right for a King to arrive in Israel.

Matthew 2:1 Now when Jesus was born in Bethlehem of Judaea in the days of Herod the king, behold, there came wise men from the east to Jerusalem,
2:2 Saying, Where is he that is born King of the Jews? for we have seen his star in the east, and are come to worship him.

A special *star,* in and of itself, can mean a variety of things. But these *wise men* (or *magi*) knew what this *star* meant, because they knew what time it was. Daniel, or Belteshazzar (as the Babylonians knew him – Daniel 1:7), was well-known in both Babylon and Persia (Dan. 2:46-48; 5:29; 6:3, 25-28). Magi from that area (the east) would have been familiar with Daniel and his writings, explaining how they knew the *time* of Christ's birth, but not the exact *place*. They had to ask where to find Him. That information was in the hands of the priests at Jerusalem, in the scroll of the prophet, Micah, where we learn that the Messiah would be born in Bethlehem (Matthew 2:1-5; Mica 5:2). The magi knew the times, and acted accordingly.

Jerusalem Christians Fled to Pella

The Christians of Jerusalem, remembering the Lord's admonition, forsook the doomed city in good time and fled to the town of Pella in the Decapolis, beyond the Jordan, in the north of Peraea, where king Herod Agrippa II., before whom Paul once stood, opened to them a safe asylum.

- Philip Schaff, History of the Christian Church, Vol. I

There are two records of Christians fleeing Jerusalem before its destruction. They come to us from around AD 330-370 by two sources, Eusebius and Epiphanius. Both were Christian bishops from that time period who relied on earlier accounts for their information. Both acknowledge the event as such, but Epiphanius also records the return to Jerusalem after its destruction by the Christians who had fled to Pella,[lxxxvi] and also refers to some of the heretical doctrines that arose in the region of Pella by the Jerusalem Christians who fled there.[lxxxvii] A mass exodus of Christians leaving Jerusalem before the Roman siege might be expected. Jesus had already warned His disciples what was going to happen:

Luke 21:20 And when ye shall see Jerusalem compassed with armies, then know that the desolation thereof is nigh.

And if they were familiar at all with Daniel 9:26 (they would have the text without the chapter and verse – those came later), then they also knew that at some point after the *anointed one* was *cut off*, that the city and the sanctuary would be destroyed.

And they left.

Preparing for the Storm

The Christians in Jerusalem understood what Jesus told them, and left before the city was destroyed. Likewise, we know what is going to happen before it happens, because Jesus already told us as well. And the events of our times are much like the first winds of an approaching hurricane. A hurricane is unpredictable, and can turn in any direction at any moment. It can also fizzle out or weaken before it hits. But those possibilities have never stopped the preparation for its arrival by those in its path as it approached. And whether this particular storm hits in our lifetime, or if it does not, the wise course is to be prepared regardless.

Jesus tells us to watch, and to pray. He tells us to endure to the end, whether to the end of our lives or to the end of the age. He expects to be taken seriously, and He knows who is paying attention, and who is not. And we are in a fix. We have work to do on our lives.

1st John 3:3 And every man that hath this hope in him purifieth himself, even as he is pure.

We are sinful. At every turn, we find ourselves confronted with another problem in the flesh. We ask forgiveness, we ask for help. Ultimately, we have to struggle with our own being, striving to follow after the Spirit in spite of ourselves. And if that is not enough, we have external difficulties thrown upon us. When Jesus said the way is hard, He meant it. So watch, pray, and endure. And His promise of escaping the coming storm will hold true. This is the best way to prepare, because it is based on His promise.

While working out our salvation (Philippians 2:12-15), it is also wise to prepare ourselves in the physical realm for the times that are coming. By AD 70, the Christians of Jerusalem had already fled to Pella.[lxxxviii] They had a place to go. Our situation is not so certain. There may be no place for us to go if we happen to be here during those times.

We saw how quickly the recent pandemic caused the global lockdown, with people in power enforcing questionable vaccines and proofs of vaccination for air travel or eating in restaurants, along with the apocalyptic horrors we witnessed during that time. We saw the governor of New York and those of other states forcing nursing homes to accept infected people into their facilities, thus exposing the weakest and most vulnerable to the virus. It seemed that they were intentionally increasing the virus death toll to puff up the numbers in order to foment fear among the masses and thereby drive them into voluntary compliance to ruling authorities.

We saw the police try to shut down churches in free nations, even as the people met outside and stayed in their cars, socially distanced as required. People were told what they were allowed to buy at the stores, and what was prohibited (most notably by the governor of Michigan). These kinds of things were taking place on a global scale. From that experience, we should be fully aware of how quickly Satan can act through his world leaders and local governing officials (his principalities and powers). The media-driven panic over Covid-19 was clearly a power-grab on a global scale, and we watched it happen. The next one may be successful. It is not unwise to maintain a state of readiness in the hour in which we are living.

The post 9/11 world has been informed by entities such as FEMA (Federal Emergency Management Agency), the Red Cross, and others to be prepared for unexpected emergencies, to include maintaining home survival kits. It would be a very good idea to hop on the Internet for a list of items you will need from one of their web sites. They won't include a gun or a weapon for protection. You have to add that yourself.[lxxxix] We would not be out of line to go the extra mile, and make preparation for food and water for several months, or even more than a year.

The period of time between the government mandating a *mark* (or identification for economic participation), and the enforcement of it against noncompliant citizens might buy some time for a measure of freedom to continue in society without taking part in its economy. But that means you would need a source for food and water outside of the economy. After the events of 2020, many have already stocked up.

Freeze-dried food with a shelf-life of over 25 years is available online. Some brands are relatively inexpensive at the moment, but as we all know, that could change overnight. Also, certain canned and dry foods from your local grocer have been known to last and retain freshness for years beyond their stamped expiration dates. So do the research, and shop around for the best prices and quality.

Location may also be a consideration. Think ahead. Consider the political climate of your area. You might want to change your environment, if possible. Property with its own well water is a plus. You will need to be close to a reliable water supply if or when things go south. Water purification kits or filters might also be a good investment.

Some companies offer mini-filters that attach to water bottles, and even allow you to drink through a straw directly from the source (lake or stream). You will also need water for cooking and to keep clean. Never discount the importance of a good bar of soap. Items for dental hygiene, as well as first-aid are also indispensable.

For the long haul, there is an abundance of books available on how to grow your own food, as well as guidebooks about edible plants in the wild. You might also purchase a book on home remedies for common ailments. I mention books because the internet can be tracked for location, and you will not want to be using a cell phone. You will probably want to avoid electrical devices altogether. Physical books are not on the grid, but you may need to inspect them and remove any microchips for tracking. Remember that our predecessors lived off the land, without doctors or dentists; and there was no toilet paper on the wagon train. Compared to the first six thousand years of human history, these measures are by no means extreme.

The magi were ready when the King was born, and their eyes saw the baby Jesus. And when the Roman armies surrounded Jerusalem, the Christians were gone. And we, too, can also be ready by drawing closer to God through prayer and abiding in His Word, while purifying our lives from sin and selfishness unto selflessness and good toward others.

And it never hurts to have some extra food and other provisions for the difficult days to come. Even if you don't use any of it, someone else may be glad you prepared. Think of the kids. And pray for them.

Notes

[i] "Does Eschatology Matter?"
https://www.bereanbiblechurch.org/transcripts/topical/does-eschatology-matter.htm

[ii] Brown-Driver-Briggs Hebrew and English Lexicon.

[iii] Seventh Day Adventist calculations have "Messiah the Prince" fulfillment at the baptism of Jesus:
https://www.adventistbiblicalresearch.org/materials/when-did-the-seventy-weeks-of-daniel-924-begin/ .
Popular evangelical teachers (Drs. David Jeremiah, John Macarthur and others) follow Sir Robert Anderson's calculations and place the fulfillment at His triumphal entry riding on a donkey:
https://www.whatsaiththescripture.com/Text.Only/pdfs/The_Coming_Prince_Text.pdf
Other calculations, like the two examples above, also assume Jesus as the fulfillment of the entire prophecy of Daniel 7:25-26, and accordingly connect the 7 weeks with the 62 weeks.

[iv] *English Standard Version*, *Lexham English Bible*, and others. Also the Spanish translation, *La Palabra de Dios para Todos*.

[v] The second most popular idea separates the Medes and Persians, making them the second and third beasts, with Greece as the fourth.

[vi] Ante-Nicene Fathers, Vol. 5, *Appendix to the Works of Hippolytus*, XIV-XV, p. 245. Hendrickson Publishers, Inc., 1994 (reprint of the American Edition by the Christian Literature Publishing Company, 1886).

[vii] From the future יְקוּמוּן (shall arise). Kiel & Delitzsch Commentary of the Old Testament, e-Sword.net, download.

[viii] Britannica online :"Rashidun"
 https://www.britannica.com/topic/Rashidun

[ix] Ibid. "Umayyad dynasty"
https://www.britannica.com/topic/Umayyad-dynasty-Islamic-history

[x] World History Encyclopedia online: "Abbasid Dynasty"
https://www.worldhistory.org/Abbasid_Dynasty/

[xi] Denmark-Norway union ran from 1524-1814.

[xii] Russia is not included as it emerged from the Byzantine Empire, the second beast (the bear) and not the fourth.

[xiii] William MacDonald, Believer's Bible Commentary, J. Vernon McGee's Thru the Bible commentary, and others

[xiv] 1 Kings 6:16; 7:50; 8:6 and others.

[xv] Leviticus 6:25; 7:1, 6. Hebrews 10:10-12; 2 Corinthians 5:19-21.

^{xvi} Albert Barnes made the same assessment over a hundred years ago: "Our translators undoubtedly understood it as referring to him who is known as the Messiah, but this is not necessarily implied in the original. All that the language fairly conveys is, 'until an anointed one.'" See Albert Barnes' Notes on the Bible for Daniel 9:25.

^{xvii} If by the 70 *sevens*, or *weeks*, Gabriel meant complete revolutions of the earth around the sun (365 ¼ days), or what we call, "solar years," then the 434 years (62 weeks) from the 20th year of Artaxerxes I takes us to 10 BC. The 360 day Jewish lunar calendar is not as constant, but adds an extra month periodically to make up for lost days that accumulate over time. My use of the term "range," in the text, is reflective of my confidence level of our accuracy in dating events of antiquity. It becomes complicated due to lack of complete information. In this case, much is based on *Ptolemy's Canon;* an ancient list of kings and when they reigned, in conjunction with astronomical events. But since that canon omits kings that reigned less than a year, absorbing them into the times of longer reigning kings, it is reasonable that the actual beginnings or endings of the reigns of the kings that are listed may not be precise. The *Canon* further obscures our precision through its use of regnal dates for the beginning of a king's reign, rather than the actual dates that the kings assumed their positions. Along with that, when we consider that our margin of error for dating the birth of Christ at roughly 4 to 7 BC is based on consensus of scholars rather than solid fact, 10 BC places us well within the ballpark for a 434 year fulfillment.

^{xviii} January 23, 1950: The Israeli Parliament declares Jerusalem Capital of Israel. Israel places its major governmental institutions in Jerusalem—parliament, supreme court, governmental offices, and prime minister's office. From CIE web site, Jerusalem Timeline: https://israeled.org/jerusalem-timeline/

^{xix} July 30, 1980: Israeli parliament passes its Fifth Basic Law, this one on Jerusalem. It states "Jerusalem, complete and united, is the capital of Israel; it is the seat of the President of the State, the Knesset, the Government and the Supreme Court. ibid.

^{xx} For more up to date information on the state of Jerusalem, see UNESCO, World Heritage Convention: https://whc.unesco.org/en/soc/4541

^{xxi} Genesis 21:22-32; 1st Kings 20:34

^{xxii} Presidents Bill Clinton, George W. Bush, Barack Obama, and Donald Trump have all worked to establish peace between Israel and other Middle Eastern nations.

[xxiii] The Temple Institute was founded in 1987, with the express purpose of rebuilding the temple in Jerusalem. https://templeinstitute.org/ According to 2nd Thessalonians 2:4 the man of sin (antichrist) will be revealed sitting in the temple of God declaring himself to be God.

[xxiv] Strong's Hebrew Dictionary, Brown-Driver-Briggs Hebrew Definitions

[xxv] Strong's Hebrew Dictionary, Brown-Driver-Briggs Hebrew Definitions

[xxvi] Some emphasize the meaning of the word, Christ, as "anointed", and many have come in the name of Jesus and claimed to be anointed. But the article for *the* (ὁ), and the capitalization of *Christ* (Χριστός) in the Greek text here in Matthew 24:5 makes it clear that Jesus is referring to Himself: *the* Christ.

[xxvii] The Believer's Bible Commentary, the Wycliffe Bible Commentary and others.

[xxviii] Had Jesus meant that the deceivers would be claiming to be Christ, it might have read more like this: *Many shall come in My name, saying they are Christ*; or *Many shall come in My name claiming to be Me*. As it stands, Jesus is speaking in the first person and is most likely referring to Himself.

[xxix] Genesis 28:13-15 provides one example. God speaks to Jacob, and through Jacob to his descendants by combining both into one.

[xxx] Isaiah 2:2-4; 11:1-9; 60:18-22

[xxxi] Strong's Greek Dictionary; Strong's Exhaustive Concordance of the Bible.

[xxxii] I highly recommend this free downloadable Bible study software (PC and MAC), which incorporates and integrates centuries of scholarly work, word studies, maps, Bible translations and more (special thanks to Rick Meyer, the creator of e-Sword). Also available for a very small price is an edition designed as an app for cell phones. You will not be disappointed.

[xxxiii] Webster's New World College Dictionary, Fourth Edition

[xxxiv] The New Foxe's Book of Martyrs provides a history of Christian persecution both inside and outside the Church. A lot of Christians were burned alive.

[xxxv] "Adel" of Indonesia relates one example from the year 2000. Read Hearts of Fire: Eight Women in the Underground Church and Their Stories of Costly Faith published by The Voice of the Martyrs.

[xxxvi] This is a profound statement. To those who disbelieve the Bible, one question: How did Jesus know that this would happen? In a statement made in passing, 2000 years ago, Jesus said that *this gospel of the kingdom* would be preached to all nations. And today there are Christians in the most remote tribes on the planet.

[xxxvii] Hitler, Pol Pot, Rwanda, the Taliban, the communist regimes of China, Cambodia, and the Soviet Union provide excellent examples of mass executions and genocide.

xxxviii *If possible.* The implication, according to some, is that it is *not* possible. However, the reality is that even *the elect* can be *deceived* on any number of fronts; hence the multiplicity of denominations of Christianity, not to mention success of certain televangelists appealing to fleshly desires. *"If possible"* may depend on the individual Christian who allows for the possibility. See also the example of Peter and Barnabas in Galatians 2:11-14.

xxxix The Greek here, *enistēmi (ἐνίστημι)* can mean either present or impending. Most English translations consider the thought to mean that the Day of Christ had already arrived. See also 2 Timothy 2:16-18.

xl Apostasy, apostate, apostates: The same Greek word and its variations are used in every instance throughout the Greek Septuagint (as translated from the Hebrew) and O. T. Apocrypha. The words always carry a meaning of departing from God. See Joshua 22:16, 19, 22; 2nd Chronicles 29:19; Job 26:13; Isaiah 30:1; Jeremiah 2:19; 3rd Maccabees 2:33. In Acts 21:21, where Paul is charged with teaching Jews to forsake the law of Moses, *apostasy* is the Greek word used.

xli Thayer's Greek Lexicon

xlii Forbidding priests to marry and proclaiming mandatory fasts was a partial apostasy within the Catholic Church by its leaders in the Middle-Ages. Any doctrine that forbids what God has allowed is called a doctrine of demons (1st Timothy 4:1-5).

xliii Benjamin Franklin, for example, was a Deist, and not a Christian, although his knowledge of God was from the Bible and the Church. Thomas Jefferson made his own Bible by cutting out the miracles of Jesus. The same man who penned the Declaration of Independence denied the power of God (2nd Tim. 3:5).

xliv Wellhausen's works are cited in many critical commentaries and in the introductory material of the more liberal study Bibles. Through the J E P D hypothesis, which cannot be checked or verified (hence, it is still merely a hypothesis – a guess), he credits the writings of the Pentateuch to four purely human sources: "J" for someone who called God, "Jehovah," "E" for someone else who called God "Elohim," "P" for writings he attributed to priests, and "D" for Deuteronomist, which he says came much later. Although these opinions have largely been discredited over the last few decades, critical scholars continue their work, inventing new narratives to remove the inspiration of Scripture and attribute its writings to the work of men. Welcome to the apostasy.

[xlv] "Liberal" is a term that was originally intended to describe those who embrace diversity. The tendency, however, is normally inclusive of views hostile to God and His Word (other religions, sinful activity as described in the Bible), leading to exclusion of the truth of the gospel. By attributing to others the authorship of Daniel, for example, they are in effect, calling Jesus a liar. Jesus affirmed Daniel as the author of the book bearing his name (Matt. 24:15).

[xlvi] The Oxford Annotated Bible, The Interpreter's Bible, the Southern Baptist's Broadman Bible Commentary (1969 edition) provide a few examples.

[xlvii] B. B. Warfield's Systematic Theology supplies one example.

[xlviii] Thayer's Greek Lexicon

[xlix] Albert Barnes' Notes on the Bible. Written during the 1800s, Barnes' held that this passage (2nd Thess. 2:4) was a reference to the church.

[l] Both Martin Luther and John Calvin viewed the papal position as antichrist, as many do to this day.

[li] Ante-Nicene Fathers, Vol. 3. Tertullian, *On the Resurrection of the Flesh*, p. 563. The New International Commentary still holds to this view as the best, though still not certain, interpretation (p. 1470).

[lii] Matthew Henry's Commentary, e-Sword edition. But the Pope cannot be the Antichrist for the simple reason that the popes, by virtue of their position and institution, acknowledge and revere God; something that the Antichrist will not do (Dan. 7:25, 11:36-37; 2nd Thess. 2:4; Rev. 13:5).

[liii] Scofield Reference Bible, 1917 edition, footnote for 2nd Thess. 2:3, p. 1272. This footnote was expanded in The New Scofield Reference Bible of 1967 in defense against other views. The Believer's Bible Commentary lists seven different views for the restrainer, but favors the Holy Spirit as the restrainer, emphasizing His title for the neuter gender (*the* Holy Spirit) and the pronoun (*He*) for the masculine (p. 2054, for this comment under the heading, *B: The Man of Sin*).

[liv] The Wycliffe Bible Commentary asks a very good question on this note: "How can the revelation of Antichrist be a sign to the church that has already been raptured?" The Wycliffe Bible Commentary, p. 1364,

[lv] Thayer's Greek Definitions, e-Sword edition.

[lvi] Theological Dictionary of the New Testament, Vol. II, p. 829.

[lvii] This is an understatement. This *hindering influence* or *holding back* is much more encompassing. It is in every hindrance and interruption occurring during the presentation of the gospel. It works in the mind of the hearer, rationalizing postponement of acting upon hearing, or through a rationale for nonbelief, or sudden interruptions in thought about other things that need to be done, etc.

It also affects the messenger of the gospel psychologically by the influence of others (perceived or real) and/or within his or her own mind through doubt or nervousness, to *hold back* from sharing the gospel. The enemy works on all levels. As we have already seen, the *restrainer* has also worked effectively in obscuring our understanding of Bible prophecy for centuries. For the creation of antichrists, however, false teaching within the church works covertly in tandem with false teaching outside the church (world religions, science falsely so called: 1st Timothy 6:20) in preparation for the unveiling of the *man of sin* when his time arrives.

[lviii] The Berean Literal Bible, Smith's Literal Translation, Literal Emphasis Translation, Godbey New Testament also have the text reading as coming up "from the midst" rather than taken "out of the way."

[lix] Screen shot from e-Sword version of the Interlinear Greek N. T.

[lx] The International Bible Commentary and the New Bible Commentary: Revised argue for a variation here of a common idiom in the ancient Greek in support of the "taken out of the way" translation for verse 7. But those opinions do not diminish the words of the actual text.

[lxi] Satan answers to both neuter and masculine forms of κατέχω in 2 Thess. 2:6-7 (see also Gen. 3:1; Rev. 12:9 references to *the serpent*).

[lxii] From *Humanist Manifesto* I: FIRST: Religious humanists regard the universe as self-existing and not created. SECOND: Humanism believes that man is a part of nature and that he has emerged as a result of a continuous process. https://americanhumanist.org/what-is-humanism/manifesto1/

[lxiii] *Parousia* is the Greek word, and also the theological term for the coming of Christ. It is used in Matthew 24:27, 1st Thess. 4:15, and 2nd Thess. 2:1.

[lxiv] See Schaff, Philip, History of the Christian Church, Vol. 3 *Ante-Nicene Christianity,* Ch. 2, "Persecution of Christianity and Christian Martyrdom," p. 33-34; 64.

[lxv] Inherited through Roman practice, the title of sovereign high priest applied to the emperor (the biblical Melchisedec also provides an example of this ancient practice). He was both the religious high priest as well as the reigning monarch. When the Roman Empire became predominantly Christian, Constantine still retained the title.

[lxvi] Christian persecution by the established "Church" during this period is very well-known and documented. Many were burned alive, tortured and killed in various ways. The High and Late Middle ages remains an open and gaping wound in the history of the church. Persecuted Christian groups include the Anabaptists, the Huguenots, the Albigenses, the Waldensians, and others.

174

lxvii From Britannica.com, *The pregeologic period:* "It is widely accepted by both geologists and astronomers that Earth is roughly 4.6 billion years old. This age has been obtained from the isotopic analysis of many meteorites as well as of soil and rock samples from the Moon by such dating methods as rubidium–strontium and uranium–lead. It is taken to be the time when these bodies formed and, by inference, the time at which a significant part of the solar system developed."

lxviii The Babylonian *Enuma Elish*, the Greek *Deucalion*, the Indian *Satapatha Brahmana*, to name a few ancient sources. But creation and flood stories are found all over the world.

lxix https://www.oldest.org/culture/family-trees/ House of Solomon royal family of Ethiopia traces its genealogy to King Solomon, as does the Lurie Family. During the so called "Neolithic Revolution" (farming, cities, pottery), human migration originated from between the Black and Caspian seas, the same location as Mt. Ararat. Genesis 10 provides invaluable information of these progenitors of what later became the nations of antiquity.

lxx Dionysius Exiguus, the Catholic monk from whom we number the years, was a little off in his calculation as to when Christ was born.

lxxi J. Vernon McGee's Thru the Bible Commentary, the Believer's Bible Commentary, the Wycliffe Bible Commentary all teach this. Also the Amplified Bible, the Good News Translation and the Contemporary English Version interpret Daniel 12:4 in this manner.

lxxii Sir Lancelot Brenton, Septuagint with Apocrypha: Greek and English

lxxiii Reuters - https://www.reuters.com/

lxxiv Brown-Driver-Briggs Hebrew and English Lexicon, and Strong's Hebrew/Chaldee Dictionary.

lxxv This one is particularly horrific. Marriage between man and woman has always been universally recognized all over the world throughout its history, and points back to God, who inaugurated the marriage of our first parents in the garden (Gen. 2:21-24).

lxxvi https://www.goodmorningamerica.com/gma3/video/11-year-trailblazing-drag-kid-desmond-amazing-58926262

lxxvii "Joe Biden: 8-year-olds should be able to decide they're transgender ... 'zero discrimination'" https://www.lifesitenews.com/news/joe-biden-endorses-telling-8-year-olds-theyre-transgender/

lxxviii Luther, Calvin, and many others from that age viewed the pope as antichrist.

lxxix The first Humanist Manifesto was published in 1933 in the United States.

lxxx Another instance is found in Matthew 24:30 and Revelation 1:7.

lxxxi The Seven Tenets of Satanism are found on the Satanic Temple's website.

[lxxxii] Rules For Radicals, by Saul Alinsky. The quote Is Alinsky's own; found on the opening page of his book.

[lxxxiii] Satan worship in an official capacity can be found the Church of Satan and the Satanic Temple in the U.S., Canada, UK, and Australia.

[lxxxiv] Spiritually speaking, cartoons like *Pete's Dragon, Dragon Tales, Barney,* etc. presenting Satan as a cute, huggable sort of creature shouldn't be taken lightly.

[lxxxv] The examples are numerous. Carrie Fisher and Peter Cushing are alive again in *Star Wars* episodes made years after their deaths. More famous is the posthumous cameo appearance of John F. Kennedy in a scene from *Forrest Gump.* But even now this has become old news. Hologram technology has advanced to such a degree that a person can appear to be in more than one place at the same time.

[lxxxvi] Epiphanius, *Tables of Weights and Measures* 54d-55a, pp. 30-31

[lxxxvii] Epiphanius, *Panarion* 29,7,7-8; 30, 2,7.

[lxxxviii] Jesus encouraged His disciples to flee persecution:
Matthew 10:23 But when they persecute you in this city, flee ye into another: for verily I say unto you, Ye shall not have gone over the cities of Israel, till the Son of man be come.

[lxxxix] Jesus did advise purchasing weapons for defense:
Luke 22:36 Then said he unto them, But now, he that hath a purse, let him take it, and likewise his scrip: and he that hath no sword, let him sell his garment, and buy one.

Bibliography

<u>Ante-Nicene Fathers</u>, 10 Volumes. Hendrickson Publishers, Inc., 1994 (reprint of the American Edition by the Christian Literature Publishing Company, 1886)

<u>Brown-Driver-Briggs Hebrew and English Lexicon,</u> Hendrickson Publishers, Inc., 2000 (reprint of the 1906 edition originally published by Houghton, Mifflin, and Co., Boston)

Brenton, Lancelot C. L. <u>Septuagint with Apocrypha: Greek and English</u> Hendrickson Publishers, 6th Printing, 1997 (Reprint of 1851 publication by Samuel Bagster & Sons, Ltd., London)

Bruce, F.F., General Editor, <u>The International Bible Commentary</u>, Zondervan Publishing House, Grand Rapids, MI, 1986, Guideposts Edition.

Epiphanius, <u>Panarion of Epiphanius of Salamis</u>, Book I. Translated by Frank Williams, Published by Brill, Leiden, Boston, 2009

Epiphanius, <u>Tables of Weights and Measures</u>, James Elmer Dean, Ed., University of Chicago, 1935

Foxe, John, <u>The New Foxe's Book of Martyrs</u>, Bridge-Logos Publishers, New Brunswick, NJ, 1997.

Green, Jay P., Sr., <u>The Interlinear Bible</u>, One Volume Edition, Jay P. Green, 1985.

Guthrie, Motyer, Stibbs, and Wiseman, <u>The New Bible Commentary: Revised</u>, Carmel, NY, Guideposts edition, 1984

Kittel, Gerhard and Friedrich Gerhard, <u>Theological Dictionary of the New Testament</u>, Vol. II, Wm. B. Eerdmans Publishing Co., Grand Rapids, MI, 1964, Tenth printing, March 1980.

MacDonald, William, <u>Believer's Bible Commentary</u>, Thomas Nelson Publishers, 1995.

McGee J. Vernon, <u>Thru the Bible with J. Vernon McGee</u>, 5 Volume Set, Thomas Nelson Publishers, Inc. 1981

<u>Nicene and Post Nicene Fathers</u> (NPNF) Hendrickson Publishers, Inc., 1994 (reprint of the American Edition by T. and T. Clark, and the Christian Literature Publishing Company, 1886-1890)

Pfeiffer, Charles F., and Harrison, Everett F., Editors, <u>The Wycliffe Bible Commentary,</u> Moody Bible Institute, Chicago, 1972

Schaff, Philip, <u>History of the Christian Church</u>, 8 Volumes, Wm. B. Eerdman's Publishing Company, 1994 (reprint of the 1910 edition, by Charles Scribner's Sons)

Scofield, C. I. <u>The Scofield Reference Bible</u>, New York, Oxford University Press, Copyright 1909, 1917, renewed 1937, 1945.

Scofield, C. I. <u>The New Scofield Reference Bible</u>, New York, Oxford University Press, 1967

<u>Strong's Exhaustive Concordance of the Bible</u>, by James A. Strong, Baker Book House, Grand Rapids, MI 1984 (reprint of the 1890 edition)

<u>Thayer's Greek-English Lexicon of the New Testament</u>, Baker Book House, Grand Rapids, MI 1984 (reprint of the 1901 edition by T. and T. Clark)

The Voice of the Martyrs, <u>Hearts of Fire: Eight Women in the Underground Church and Their Stories of Costly Faith</u>, Bartlesville, OK, VOM Books, 2003, 2015.

Internet Sources

<u>Albert Barnes' Notes on the Bible</u>, 1884. e-Sword.net, download

American Humanist Association: *Humanist Manifesto I.* (this primary source offers insight into the Humanistic influence on global politics and the Humanist reasoning for pressing toward a secular global society). https://americanhumanist.org/what-is-humanism/manifesto1/

Britannica.com
https://www.britannica.com/

Center for Israel Education (CIE): *Jerusalem Timeline:*
https://israeled.org/jerusalem-timeline/

Depuydt, Leo: *"More Valuable than All Gold": Ptolemy's Royal Canon and Babylonian Chronology*
https://www.journals.uchicago.edu/doi/abs/10.2307/1359818?journalCode=jcs

GMA (Good Morning America): *The 11-year-old trailblazing drag kid 'Desmond is Amazing*
https://www.goodmorningamerica.com/gma3/video/11-year-trailblazing-drag-kid-desmond-amazing-58926262

LIFESITE: *Joe Biden: 8-year-olds should be able to decide they're transgender … 'zero discrimination'*
https://www.lifesitenews.com/news/joe-biden-endorses-telling-8-year-olds-theyre-transgender/

Kiel & Delitzsch Commentary of the Old Testament, 1864
e-Sword.net, download
Myers, Rick: e-Sword® Copyright © 2022 —. https://www.e-sword.net (free downloadable Bible with multiple translations, commentaries, word studies, and many other reference works from the public domain or charitably contributed by their sources)

Popkik, Barry *"Never talk about religion or politics" (etiquette rule)*
https://www.barrypopik.com/index.php/new_york_city/entry/never_talk_about_religion_or_politics_etiquette_rule

Shea, William H.: *When Did the Seventy Weeks of Daniel 9:24 Begin?* Seventh Day Adventist Biblical Research Institute:
https://www.adventistbiblicalresearch.org/materials/when-did-the-seventy-weeks-of-daniel-924-begin/

Sir Robert Anderson (1841-1918): The Coming Prince. The full text of Anderson's book can be found at the *What Saith the Scripture* web site at this link:
https://www.whatsaiththescripture.com/Text.Only/pdfs/The_Coming_Prince_Text.pdf

The Temple Institute: https://templeinstitute.org/ (for latest information on this organization's plans and progress in restoring the temple in Jerusalem)

World History Encyclopedia online
https://www.worldhistory.org/

J C Farris graduated Summa Cum Laude from Saint Leo College (now Saint Leo University). He holds a BA in religious studies and has continued graduate studies at Southeastern Baptist Theological Seminary. He served as a pastor in Virginia for seven years and has studied biblical prophecy for over forty years.
His other books include *Ruth: A Living Parable of Jesus Christ* (as well as a Spanish version), and *God's Economy: The Tithe and New Testament Giving*.

Contact at Farris-JC@outlook.com

The cover art for this book, *When We Are*, is taken from Wikimedia Commons and is in the public domain. The photograph is attributed to E. Benjamin Andrews, from Volume 5 of his work, *History of the United States*, published by Charles Scribner's Sons, New York. 1912. The three ships pictured are replicas of the Pinta, the Niña, and the Santa Maria from the historic voyage of Christopher Columbus; the first of many such vessels that would later circle the globe, and in so doing, fulfill the prophecy of the Fourth Beast of Daniel 7.

https://commons.wikimedia.org/wiki/File:1893_Nina_Pinta_Santa_Maria_replicas.jpg